Essential RenderMan®

Ian Stephenson

Essential RenderMan®

Second Edition

 Springer

Ian Stephenson, DPhil
National Centre for Computer Animation
Bournemouth University, Poole, UK

British Library Cataloguing in Publication Data
A catalogue record for this book is available from the British Library

Library of Congress Control Number: 2006922751
ISBN 978-1-84628-344-4   eISBN 978-1-84628-800-5

Printed on acid-free paper

9 8 7 6 5 4 3 2 1

Springer Science+Business Media
springer.com

Contents

Preface

When I wrote Essential RenderMan *fast* in 2002 it didn't seem that I was writing about a moving target. The RenderMan API is a standard, and hence doesn't change radically from release to release. However, once you start writing things down they seem to change far more quickly than you expect.

No sooner had the book gone to press than two important renderers disappeared—BMRT and Entropy were both withdrawn as Exluna became a part of Nvidia. While these systems are missed, new comers Aqsis and 3DLight have both grown in strength and popularity (and have contributed images to this new edition), providing many users with their first experiences of RenderMan.

Global Illumination is the biggest technical development. In 2002, GI was still largely missing from the RenderMan API. Some renderers supported it, but in varying degrees and with different APIs. Pixar's inclusion of GI in PRMan 11 announced that GI was ready for feature film production, and provided a standard interface which other implementations could maintain compatability with. Four years later and GI is *almost* a standard feature of RenderMan, and can be included in this second edition. I say *almost* as things are still changing—Integrating GI with SL shaders is a tricky job, and we are still learning how to do it. Each new release of a renderer adds some extension which may be more widely adopted, or may fade away when we realise it isn't such a good idea after all.

The biggest change in the new edition is therefore the addition of a chapter on GI. It can only consider the core features of RenderMan GI, as each implementation still has its own unique quirks, but should provide a starting point for your own GI experiments. Everything else has been tweaked, edited and re-rendered, with extra tips, tricks, and warnings to help you through your first weeks of RenderMan. Thanks to all of those who provided images for the new edition, and to everyone at Pixar, Sitex Graphics (Scott—Who got married), DotC Software (Rick and Cheryl—Who became grandparents), Aqsis (Paul), 3DLight (Aghiles and crew), and ART for getting the software out there so that I can write about it. Thanks to everyone at the NCCA, including John Vince (who retired).

Special thanks to Amanda (who got married to me!). By the time you read this we will also be parents . . . I guess a lot *does* change in four years.

Part 1
General Overview

Chapter 1
What is RenderMan?

The first question that needs to be answered is "What exactly is RenderMan?" Contrary to the common missuse of the term within the animation and effects industry, RenderMan is not the renderer developed and used by Pixar to produce their animated movies. In fact RenderMan is not a piece of software at all.

RenderMan is a rendering API. What this means in practice is that RenderMan defines how animation and modeling software, like SoftImage or Maya, should talk to rendering software, as in Figure 1.1. The rendering software receives instructions from the modeler that describe the scene and from these commands it generates images. This separation of modeling from rendering benefits developers of modeling software, developers of renderers, and end users. The API was developed by Pixar in the late 1980s at a time when they were developing custom rendering hardware. They were concerned that as wide a range of users as possible should

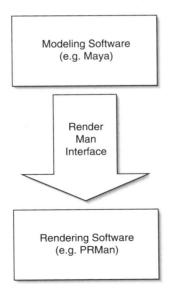

FIGURE 1.1. A Rendering API

be able to make use of their system, and hence entered into discussion with other major graphics companies. The result of these negotiations was the publication of the RenderMan standard. The idea was that anyone could develop modeling software which could talk to Pixar's new hardware. In addition, anyone could build a rendering system which conformed to the standard—The standard being designed to avoid being directly tied to any particular rendering technique or implementation. Any modeler that conformed to the standard would be able to render its images using any renderer that conformed to the standard.

Ideally, users would be able to select the modeler that best suited their needs, and match it to a renderer with an appropriate set of features, as in Figure 1.2. Software developers could focus on the area of the animation pipeline in which they excelled, and let others provide the tools required for other tasks. Technical directors who developed skills in RenderMan would be able to apply their expertise even when they have upgraded to a new software package, or moved between studios using different rendering systems.

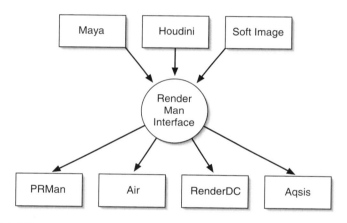

FIGURE 1.2. Mix and match toolsets

Unfortunately, owing to the politics of commercial production and software development, this situation did not materialize. Pixar's hardware failed to become commercially viable, though they did produce a very successful software implementation of their renderer which also conformed to the RenderMan standard. This software is known as PhotoRealistic RenderMan, or PRMan. However, for many years no other RenderMan compliant renderers were available. In fact, RenderMan became synonymous with PRMan.

Though the PRMan software has always been considered to be excellent, it is rather expensive. Only a few companies producing high quality film work could afford PRMan, and as a result few modeling packages made the effort to provide good support for RenderMan renderers.

Things began to change with the release of Blue Moon Rendering Tools (BMRT). When this renderer was made available at very low cost, RenderMan became accessable to a new group of users who could never have afforded PRMan. This opening up of RenderMan led to increased support and interest in the API.

BMRT is no longer available, but in recent years, many renders that claim some degree of RenderMan compatibility have become available. Each of these provides a different set of strengths and features such as global illumination, speed, portability, or simply cost. Many of these renderers are commercial, while others are available as free downloads from the authors' websites.

Access to RenderMan from animation packages has also improved. Some packages have support for RenderMan renderers built in, but most require a plug-in of some kind. The style of these plug-ins varies, as does their cost and quality.

Though the RenderMan API has been in use for many years, it is perhaps now more relevant than ever. It has wide support, and production houses worldwide are using high quality RenderMan compliant renderers. RenderMan is at last starting to realize its potential as the PostScript of 3D.

Chapter 2
Is RenderMan for Me?

In principle, it should be possible to use a RenderMan compliant renderer from a compatible animation package with virtually no knowledge of the rendering API. In practice, however, this is rarely the case, and at the very least an understanding of the general architecture is invaluable. Though we would like to be able to treat rendering as something that "just works," even the best rendering systems benefit from a little user intervention.

Rendering is a complex part of the computer imaging process. RenderMan gives the user control over almost all aspects of this process and hence a full understanding can take many years to acquire. To use a RenderMan renderer to its full potential on a project requires the same investment in time and effort as you might expect to spend learning an animation and modeling package. Fortunately, it is possible to obtain useful results from a more limited effort.

While the full details of the RenderMan API are complex, the structure is simple and a new user can rapidly gain enough experience to make minor modifications to scenes which have been generated by other means, for example, changing the color of an object, or re-rendering a scene at a higher resolution. Manually modifying a scene can enable access to the more powerful facilitates available in the renderer that may not be supported by a particular animation package. Inspecting the scenes generated by your modeler prior to rendering is a powerful debugging technique.

This book assumes no specific knowledge of rendering, but some background experience of computer graphics techniques is useful. Limited programming experience is required but in most cases the complexity of code required to produce useful results is far simpler than found in even the most basic programming books and courses—most of our programs will be ten lines of code or less. Basic knowledge of MEL or a other scripting language should provide adequate background experience.

Users with more programming experience should be able to generate scenes from their own programs within a few weeks, allowing the development of custom modeling software without worrying about how the images will be rendered.

RenderMan's most powerful feature is the control it gives over the appearance of surfaces. Virtually any kind of surface texture, shading, or deformation can be requested, and applied to any object. Defining high quality surfaces can be a

complex task, taking in physics, mathematics, programming, and aesthetic con-
siderations, but in most cases the requirements of a particular surface for a single
shot are far simpler, and even a novice user can produce interesting results with a
little practice.

Though the mathematics of rendering can be somewhat complex most of this
is hidden within the rendering system itself, and with a few exceptions should not
be an obstacle. This book is aimed at a user who may not yet be technically skilled
but is prepared to become more involved in technical issues in order to produce
images of the highest quality.

Chapter 3
An Overview of the RenderMan System

When the RenderMan standard was first proposed, computer graphics was still an esoteric topic of research practised by skilled proponents. The typical expectation was that these users would be writing their own programs to generate geometry, probably in the C programming language. As a result, the first release of the RenderMan API defined a set of C functions which could be called by modeling programs to pass instructions to a renderer.

While the C API is an appropriate mechanism for researchers to use when communicating to a renderer, it rapidly became clear that for commercial production, a more flexible mechanism was required. Users need to be able to generate a scene on one machine, and then pass it to the renderer of their choice running on a renderfarm. For this reason the RenderMan Interface Byte stream (RIB) file format was introduced.

A modeling program will still make calls to the C API internally, but rather than actually rendering, these will typically create a RIB file. These RIB files can then be examined, modified, and finally passed to a stand-alone rendering program, perhaps running on a completely different machine.

The interface between the modeler and the renderer is therefore typically in the form of a RIB file. As a result, it is probably reasonable to say that the RIB file format represents the RenderMan standard—a RenderMan compliant modeler writes RIBs while a RenderMan compliant renderer reads RIBs.

While it is perfectly possible to simply rely on a modeling package to generate RIBs, a great deal of power and flexibility can be gained from even limited knowledge of the RIB format. RIB files are generally stored as text and can easily be created or modified by a user. Though they do tend to contain rather a lot of numbers representing points in 3D space which are hard to interpret manually, the overall structure consists of a list of simple commands which can easily be identified and understood. Even when working entirely within the modeling package, the interface typically makes reference to RIB level features.

Though RIBs define the geometry of a scene, RenderMan distinguishes between the shape of an object and its surface detail. Most objects are geometrically simple, and can be represented by very primitive geometry. For example, an orange is basically a sphere. However, real objects differ from typical computer-generated objects in that on closer examination they display complex surface textures, and interact with light in a range of interesting fashions. A real orange is not perfectly round, it has pitting in the skin and an interesting waxy reaction to light.

While all modern rendering systems provide the user ways to control the surface properties of an object, the RenderMan standard goes further by defining a highly complex and flexible system where the surface properties of an object are defined by "Shaders." These take the form of short pieces of computer code written in a RenderMan specific language called SL—short for Shading Language. A renderer will typically be supplied with a program to convert shaders written in this language into a format which that particular renderer can use. This is known as the shader compiler.

When a surface is defined in a RIB file, it is simply marked as having a particular shader attached. When the scene is rendered, the renderer will look for that shader, and use the code contained within it to calculate the appearance of the surface. The ability to have such fine control over the appearance of a surface is what that makes RenderMan renderers so powerful. On major projects which use RenderMan the job of shader writer may fully occupy several highly skilled members of the production crew. An understanding of shader writing is the key component in claiming to be able to "use RenderMan."

The RenderMan pipeline is summarized by Figure 3.1.

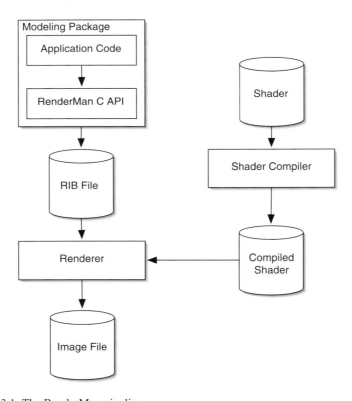

FIGURE 3.1. The RenderMan pipeline

Chapter 4
What do I Need?

The computing system used by Pixar to render their films has thousands of processors, and is one of the most powerful clusters in existence. The cost of software licenses for those machines would be outside the reach of all but the largest of studios. However, at the other end of the scale, all the examples in this book can be rendered with free software on low specification machines. A faster machine will reduce the time you have to wait, and more expensive software may generate a better-looking image, but the rendering process is otherwise identical. The information in this book applies equally to all the renderers, except where noted.

While having access to modeling software capable of interacting with RenderMan will be helpful, it is not necessary to make use of this book.

Hardware

Traditionally SGI workstations were used for the kind of highend work that RenderMan is associated with, but more recently these have been replaced by Linux and Windows machines. With Apple's move to the Unix-based MacOS X, their systems are also starting to attract interest from production studios. The underlying hardware and operating system has little direct impact on the rendering process and all of these platforms support RenderMan compatable renderers. However, the scripting and networking facilities of the UNIX-based systems still make them the preferred choice for experienced users.

The rendering process is a CPU-intensive task, which is little affected by other parameters of the machine it is running on. A fast CPU is therefore a major asset, but all of the scenes in this book may be rendered in a reasonable amount of time on current hardware. As the complexity of scenes increases, more memory may be required to render the scene efficiently. Memory can be particularly critical when global illumination is being used, but this should not be a problem when simply learning about the API. In extreme cases where very large scenes are being rendered on multiple machines, network architecture, and disk input/output (i/o) bandwidth become significant issues but these are of little concern to the new user.

Though the machine used to generate the images simply requires CPU power and memory, at some point you are going to view the images produced on screen. When viewing images, ensure that your graphics card is in 24-bit mode ("millions of colors"). While a lower color depth may give a rough idea as to the general layout of the image, any fine detail will be lost, making quality work impossible.

Rendering Software

In order to work through the examples in this book and to produce your own images, you will need a RenderMan compatable renderer. Exactly which one is right for you depends on the needs and budget of the work you are aiming to produce. Fortunately, one of the key things about RenderMan is that you can start small, learn a little, and then switch software as required. RenderMan provides a common API, so when you learn to use one of these renderers you are learning about all the others too.

At the time of writing the following RenderMan compatable renderers are available:

PhotoRealistic RenderMan (PRMan)	www.pixar.com
RenderDotC	www.dotcsw.com.
AIR	www.sitexgraphics.com
Aqsis	www.aqsis.org
ART RenderDrive	www.art-render.com
Angel	www.dctsystems.co.uk
3Delight	www.3delight.com
Pixie	sourceforge.net/projects/pixie/

Summary

As RenderMan is an API rather than a renderer, software and hardware is available in a range of forms to suit virtually every kind of user. All of these renderers should be able to render the examples used in this book, with a few minor exceptions. If you are able to install more than one, this will allow you to compare their relative merits and help you understand how RenderMan makes working with multiple renderers (and modelers) practical. Production notes, detailing specific issues which might arise as you work through this book using some of the renderers listed above are available from the books website, along with the code for most of the examples presented.

Chapter 5
How to Use This Book

This book is divided into three parts. Part 1 which you've already read, gives a general overview of the RenderMan architecture. By now you should have a good idea how the various parts of RenderMan fit together, and how it operates within a production pipeline. The remaining two parts discuss the creation of geometry and shading.

Part 2 considers geometry. We start with a simple five-line RIB file, and learn how to specify increasingly complex objects, from spheres and cones, through to complex free-form surfaces, hair, and particle systems. Once you've got to grips with RIB, you'll learn how this knowledge can be used from the C programming language. In addition to the actual shape of the objects themselves, Part 2 also includes details of how colors and shaders are attached to objects, how the camera is setup, and information on lighting your scene. Part 3 introduces you to writing shaders. Initially, we look at how the standard shaders operate, and progress by adding increasingly complex patterns to surfaces. We examine how objects may be given a more organic feel, through the use of noise, and use displacement shaders to emboss patterns onto objects. The topic of antialiasing is discussed; we develop surfaces which interact with light in unique ways, and new kind of lights which shine in interesting patterns. Finally, we look at how Global Illumination has been added to the RenderMan API.

Though there is necessarily an overlap between Parts 2 and 3, it should be possible to read each part independently. If you are interested in generating or modifying geometry, you can read only Part 2, while if you want to learn about shader writing quickly then you can skip ahead to Part 3, referring back to Part 2 as required. Both Parts 2 and 3 include numerous worked examples. Having read each chapter, you should render the examples contained within it using at least one renderer. All of the code in the book can be obtained from the book's website. The examples should be modified to verify their behavior, and explore the ideas introduced

This book is not intended to provide an exhaustive reference to the RenderMan API. It is intended as a tutorial, giving you a start into the RenderMan world. It introduces the concepts, and shows you how to make use of them in a practical fashion. In many cases, there are additional options or subtleties which are ignored for the sake of clarity. Most chapters include a section describing some of the related commands and functions which you might like to investigate further. Details of these commands along with other more general information on rendering can be found in a number of more advanced books which are listed in the bibliography. These should be referred to for more technically detailed information, once you're comfortable with the basic ideas.

Part 2
Geometry

Geometry is presented to the renderer either through a RIB file or the C API. These are closely related, and once you have learnt one, it is relatively simple to use the other. However, as the issues of C programming would only make the discussion of RenderMan more complex, we will at first restrict ourselves to using RIB. The C API will be briefly introduced in a later chapter, on the basis that proficient programmers will be able to cope with the required leap. Non programmers should simply skip this chapter.

Rather than attempt to cover each class of commands in turn, and provide a full reference, we will start with a simple scene and extend it, introducing new concepts and commands as required. The fine details of some commands will be omitted where they are not required, as they can easily be looked up in the reference texts once the basic concepts are mastered.

The API will be introduced by a series of increasingly complex examples. Each listing will be accompanied by a figure, so the code and resultant image can easily be compared. Each chapter concludes with a list of related commands which are more complex to use, or simply less useful. These are intended as suggestions for further study which you can choose to investigate or ignore as required.

You should attempt to render and extend the examples in each chapter, as this is the only method by which familiarity can be gained with the rendering process. Except where noted, all the examples should work equally well regardless of the renderer you use.

Chapter 6
A Simple Scene

Introduction

Perhaps the hardest part of using any package is actually generating your first image. In this section we will produce a simple scene by creating a RIB file and passing it to a renderer. In doing so, you will learn about the basic structure of a RIB file, and gain the practical experience needed to progress further. This will form the basis of the more complex examples in later chapters.

Making a RIB

In production, RIB files are often stored in a compressed form to save disk space, but for our purposes we can simply store RIBs as text files. RIB files for high-quality frames can be several gigabytes in size, but basic images can be produced with only a few lines of text. One of the simplest possible scenes is a single sphere in the centre of the screen. The RIB for this is in Listing 6.1, and the resultant image is shown in Figure 6.1.

Listing 6.1 A minimal scene.

```
#min.rib - a minimal scene
Display "min.tiff" "file" "rgba"
Projection "perspective"
WorldBegin
    Translate 0 0 2
    Sphere 1 -1 1 360
WorldEnd
```

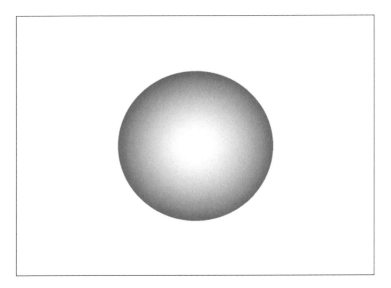

FIGURE 6.1. A minimal scene

The RIB file contains a list of commands for the renderer. Typically these will be positioned at the start of a line, and may be followed by a number of parameters. These parameters are separated by spaces, and may be split across several lines if necessary to make the file more readable.

You should type this RIB into the computer using any text editor (such as NotePad, TextEdit, or Kate) and save it to disk. Though any file name could be used, as this is one of the smallest possible RIB files we will call it "min.rib."

What goes in a RIB?

We will now examine the contents of min.rib.

#comment

Anything which follows a # character up until the end of line, is ignored by the renderer. You can therefore use that space to add any information which might be useful to someone reading the RIB file. When modeling programs generate RIB files they often use comments to indicate which object in the scene is currently being described. In this case we have added a line which includes the name of the file, and a brief description of the scene's contents.

Display

The real work of this RIB file starts with a `Display` command indicating that we want to create a file called `min.tiff`, containing RGB (red green blue) color information. We have also requested the A (alpha) channel which contains transparency information. This allows us to identify which parts of the scene contain objects and which are background. In print, the background is drawn as white, while when viewed onscreen the background may be drawn differently.

Replacing "`file`" with "`framebuffer`" will display the image directly on the screen. Specific renderers may support additional output types, which will be listed in the renderers' own documentation.

Projection

The line beginning `Projection` tells the renderer that we want to use a standard perspective projection—Far away things will be drawn smaller than close up things. A particular renderer may support other projections, but most rendering uses this standard projection.

WorldBegin and WorldEnd

Having set up the renderer, telling it how to draw, and where to store the results, we can start telling it about the things to be drawn. The command `WorldBegin` informs the renderer that the setup phase is complete, and it should prepare to draw. The related command at the end of the file `WorldEnd` informs it that the scene is finished, and it can write out the final image.

Translate and Sphere

Between `WorldBegin` and `WorldEnd` we define the objects that we want in our scene. In this case we have a single sphere, declared with the `Sphere` command, and positioned using the `Translate` command. Both of these will be covered in greater detail in the following chapters.

Rendering a RIB

Having created a RIB file which describes a simple scene, we now want to turn the RIB into an image by rendering it. Most rendering is done from the command line rather than from a GUI so open a command prompt or shell and change to the directory in which you have created min.rib. It should then be possible to render the scene by simply typing the render command followed by the name of the RIB file.

The command needed to render the scene depends on the renderer you are using:

PRMan	`prman min.rib`
Aqsis	`aqsis min.rib`
RenderDotC	`renderdc min.rib`
Angel	`angel min.rib`
3Delight	`renderdl min.rib`
Air	`air min.rib`

Refer to the documentation for your renderer to check what this command should be.

If all goes well then the file "`min.tiff`" should be created, and can be viewed using the image viewer of your choice. Depending on the renderer some diagnostics may also be printed, but for a successful render these are typically minimal.

Troubleshooting

If the file `min.tiff` is not created then something has gone wrong. A likely cause is simply that the rendering command has not been found. Check that you are using the correct command for your renderer, and that the renderer is correctly installed. You may need to set up the PATH environment variable to tell the shell where the renderer is installed.

If the render is being found, check that the file min.rib exists and is in the current directory. Make sure you have permission to write to the current directory so that the image file can be created.

If these do not solve the problem then you are probably getting an error message from the renderer such as "`Unknown Keyword`," "`Unknown Token`," or "`Parse Error`." These indicate an error in the RIB file, and may also give a line number. Check that you have entered the RIB commands correctly.

Summary

```
#This is a comment
```
Lines beginning with # are comments.
```
Display "name" "outputType" "rgba"
```
Specifies where the results should be sent and what information should be included in those results.

```
Projection "perspective"
```
How 3D space should be transformed into a 2D image.

```
WorldBegin
WorldEnd
```
Mark the beginning and end of the scene.

Chapter 7
Moving Things Around

Introduction

Having created a basic framework for our scene we need to be able to orient and position objects within it. In this chapter we will see how you can use transformations to move objects, resize them and rotate them, both individually and in groups.

Positioning Objects

The RIB file defines a 3D world which is initially empty. The first thing within that world is the camera, and the position of everything else is specified in terms of its relationship to that camera. In "`min.rib`" we created a single sphere, and moved it using a `Translate` command. Had we not moved it, it would have been centered around the camera. The command used was `Translate 0 0 2` indicating that the sphere was moved 0 units right, 0 units up and 2 units into the screen.

`Translate` is one of a group of commands known as transforms, which are used to position objects. These apply to everything that follows them, so the `Translate` command in min.rib appears before the `Sphere` command, which is on the following line. We could move the sphere left by adding the command `Translate −1 0 0` after the current `Translate` and before the `Sphere` as shown in Listing 7.1 and Figure 7.1. The two `Translate`'s are applied so that the sphere is moved both two units back, and one unit left.

Listing 7.1 Moving objects around.

```
#left.rib
Display "left.tiff" "file" "rgba"
Projection "perspective"

WorldBegin
    #move everything back 2 units
    Translate 0 0 2

    #Everything that follows is one unit left
    Translate −1 0 0
    Sphere 1 −1 1 360
WorldEnd
```

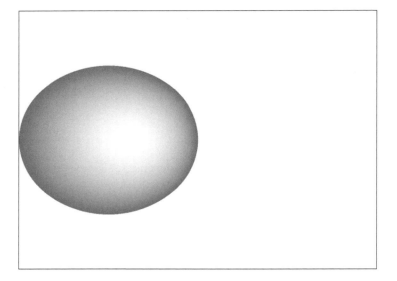

FIGURE 7.1. Moving objects around

If you want to display two spheres, you could do so using the commands shown in Listing 7.2, which uses a Translate to place the first sphere on the left, and a second Translate to move the second sphere right. However, Figure 7.2 shows that rather than displaying one sphere on the left and the other on the right as might be expected, this displays one on the left and one in the centre. The thing we have overlooked is that transforms apply to everything that follows them, so the first Translate moves the first sphere to the left but it also moves the second sphere left, and the second Translate only moves it back as far as the middle.

Listing 7.2 Multiple transforms.

```
#transform.rib
Display "transform.tiff" "file" "rgba"
Projection "perspective"

WorldBegin
    #move everything back 2 units
    Translate 0 0 2

    #Everything that follows is one unit left
    Translate -1 0 0
    Sphere 1 -1 1 360

    #Everything that follows is one unit right
    Translate 1 0 0
    Sphere 1 -1 1 360
WorldEnd
```

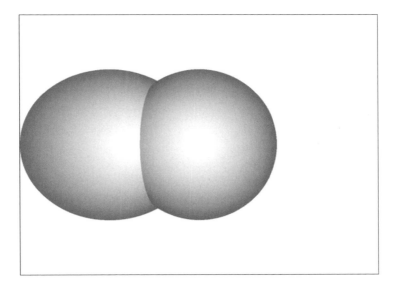

FIGURE 7.2. Multiple transforms

Grouping Transforms

While we could simply use `Translate 2 0 0` to move the second sphere further right, this would be tedious and difficult to keep track of in more complex scenes. If you were to reposition the first sphere you would have to adjust the second translation to keep the second sphere still.

A better solution to this problem would be through the use of RenderMan's "hierarchical graphics state." Basically, we can remember where we were and go back to it later. This is done using the commands `TransformBegin` and `TransformEnd`. `TransformBegin` remembers all the transformations that have been declared previously, while `TransformEnd` restores the state back to what it was at the previous `TransformBegin`. For example:

```
TransformBegin
     Translate −1 0 0
     Sphere 1 −1 1 360
TransformEnd
```

draws a sphere offset to the left, but leaves things exactly as they were before we started. If we now translate right and draw a sphere it will appear on the right rather than just back in the middle as shown in Figure 7.3 and Listing 7.3.

Listing 7.3 Grouping transforms.

```
#beginend.rib
Display "beginend.tiff" "file" "rgba"
Projection "perspective"
WorldBegin
    #move everything back 2 units
    Translate 0 0 2

    TransformBegin
        #Everything that follows is one unit left
        Translate −1 0 0
        Sphere 1 −1 1 360
    TransformEnd
    #Now we're back in the middle...
    TransformBegin
        #Everything that follows is one unit right
        Translate 1 0 0
        Sphere 1 −1 1 360
    TransformEnd
WorldEnd
```

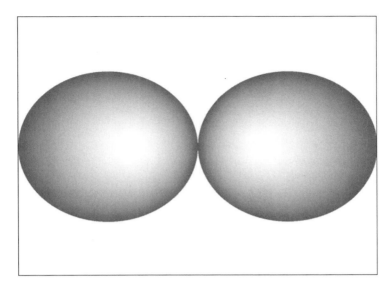

FIGURE 7.3. Grouping transforms

Using Hierarchical Transforms

While this may seem a convoluted method of defining transforms, it allows parts of the RIB to be grouped into logical blocks that reflect how elements of the scene are connected together. This becomes more important when we use more complex transformations.

For example, let us suppose you decide to use spheres to create a basic character. The character's head can be defined as a sphere. To this, we need to add two ears – also spheres – as in Figure 7.4. Listing 7.4 shows how one ear is translated left, while the other is translated right. They are then positioned on top of his head by a single translate applied to both.

Listing 7.4 A head with ears.

```
#ears.rib
Display "ears.tiff" "file" "rgba"
Projection "perspective"
WorldBegin
    #move everything back
    Translate 0 0 3

    #Head
    Sphere 1 −1 1 360
```

(*Continued*)

```
    TransformBegin
        #Ears
        Translate 0 1.3 0
        TransformBegin
            #Left Ear
            Translate -0.75 0 0
            Scale 0.5 0.5 0.5
            Sphere 1 -1 1 360
        TransformEnd

        TransformBegin
            #Right Ear
            Translate 0.75 0 0
            Scale 0.5 0.5 0.5
            Sphere 1 -1 1 360
        TransformEnd
    TransformEnd
WorldEnd
```

FIGURE 7.4. A head with ears

We have made the ears from spheres, but scaled them to make them smaller. The command for scaling is Scale and it takes three parameters allowing objects to be scaled by varying amounts in the x, y and z directions. While the ears are scaled equally in all directions, to create a nose we want a sphere which is elongated away from the head. This corresponds to the z-axis, and hence we make the third parameter of Scale slightly larger, as in Listing 7.5. Note that we do not have to worry about the translations we have applied to the ears, as these are within transform blocks. The TransformBegin and TransformEnd commands allow us to position the nose relative to the head, rather than the ears.

To make this stretching of the nose more obvious in Figure 7.5, we have rotated the whole head with the Rotate command. Rotation is specified by an angle through which to turn, and a line to rotate about. We want to rotate the head 45° about the vertical (*y*) axis, so we specify a vector of 0,1,0.

Listing 7.5 A scaled nose.

```
#head.rib
Display "head.tiff" "file" "rgba"
Projection "perspective"
WorldBegin
    #move everything back
    Translate 0 0 3

    #Rotate 45 degrees about the Y axis
    Rotate 45 0 1 0

    #Head
    Sphere 1 -1 1 360

    TransformBegin
        #Ears
        Translate 0 1.3 0
        TransformBegin
            #Left Ear
            Translate -0.75 0 0
            Scale 0.5 0.5 0.5
            Sphere 1 -1 1 360
        TransformEnd

        TransformBegin
            #Right Ear
            Translate 0.75 0 0
            Scale 0.5 0.5 0.5
            Sphere 1 -1 1 360
        TransformEnd
    TransformEnd

    TransformBegin
        #Nose
        Translate 0 0 -1.1
        Scale 0.3 0.3 0.5
        Sphere 1 -1 1 360
    TransformEnd
WorldEnd
```

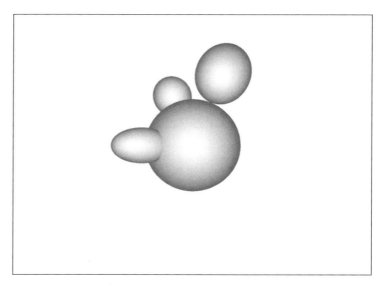

FIGURE 7.5. A scaled nose

Though the mechanism of specifying transformations seems strange, it allows groups of commands to be treated as blocks. The nose is currently modeled by a scaled sphere, but it could be replaced by something more complex, which itself contained transforms, without affecting the rest of the RIB. The nose block draws the nose relative to the head. We can then position the head relative to the body, as in Listing 7.6. We can do this without worrying about the ears or the nose, as they always follow the head. When we position the head, the nose and ears move with it, as seen in Figure 7.6.

Listing 7.6 Putting the head on a body.

```
#body.rib
Display "body.tiff" "file" "rgba"
Projection "perspective"
WorldBegin
    #move everything back
    Translate 0 0 2.5
    Translate 0 -0.75 0

    TransformBegin
        Translate 0 1.3 0
        Scale 0.5 0.5 0.5
        Rotate -30 0 1 0

        #Head
        Sphere 1 -1 1 360
```

```
            TransformBegin
                #Ears
                Translate 0 1.3 0
                TransformBegin
                     #Left Ear
                     Translate −0.75 0 0
                     Scale 0.5 0.5 0.5
                     Sphere 1 −1 1 360
                TransformEnd

                TransformBegin
                     #Right Ear
                     Translate 0.75 0 0
                     Scale 0.5 0.5 0.5
                     Sphere 1 −1 1 360
                TransformEnd
            TransformEnd

            TransformBegin
                #Nose
                Translate 0 0 −1.1
                Scale 0.3 0.3 0.5
                Sphere 1 −1 1 360
            TransformEnd
        TransformEnd

        #Body
        Sphere 1 −1 1 360
WorldEnd
```

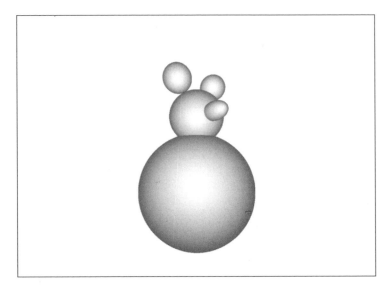

FIGURE 7.6. Putting the head on a body

A simple rule to remember is that transforms are applied from the centre outwards, so the nose is specified, and then scaled and positioned in relation to the head. The head itself is positioned relative to the body, which is positioned relative to the camera.

Summary

```
Translate x y z
Scale x y z
Rotate angle x y z
TransformBegin
TransformEnd
```

Related Commands

Identity

This command resets the current transformation back to the way it was at WorldBegin.

Transform a b c d e f g h i j k l m n o p
ConcatTransform a b c d e f g h i j k l m n o p

These allow transformations to be specified as a 4 by 4 homogeneous matrix. This format is more complex than the simple commands, but allows any combination of scales, rotates, translations, and other transformations to be specified by a single command. An introduction to homogeneous coordinate systems can be found in most computer graphics books.

Chapter 8
Simple Surfaces

Introduction

RenderMan supports a broad range of surface types, capable of reproducing virtually any shape. However, the more general surfaces can be difficult to use when you are constructing RIB files by hand. In many cases, interesting scenes can be constructed from simple geometric shapes such as spheres, cones, and cylinders which can be rendered with the minimum of effort. In this chapter we'll examine some RenderMan commands to render these kinds of objects.

Spheres

We have already used the `Sphere` command in our scenes, allowing us to set up basic renders, and experiment with transformations. So far, however, we have avoided examining the command itself in any detail. If you consider that `Sphere` takes four parameters it should become apparent that it is capable of more flexibility than might first be thought.

The first parameter of `Sphere` specifies the radius—that is, the size of the sphere. While this is geometrically identical to a scaled sphere of fixed radius, the resulting image can be different when shading is taken into account. For now you can simply choose whichever method of sizing your sphere is most convenient. To position the sphere you must use `Translate`, as spheres are always created at the origin.

The second and third parameters of the `Sphere` command allow you to clip the bottom and top of the sphere, creating a ring. Any part of the sphere below the second parameter or above the third is removed. For example, the command `Sphere 2 -0.5 1 360` would draw a sphere of radius two with most of the bottom removed, and a little of the top clipped, as shown in Listing 8.1 and Figure 8.1. Top and bottom are with respect to the z-axis, which normally points

Listing 8.1 Clipping a sphere.

```
#clipped.rib
Display "clipped.tiff" "file" "rgba"
Projection "perspective"
WorldBegin
    Rotate -90 1 0 0
    Translate 0 -4 0
    Sphere 2 -0.5 1 360
WorlldEnd
```

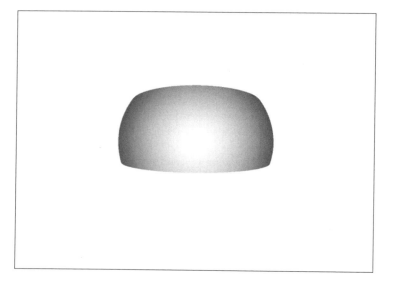

FIGURE 8.1. Clipping a sphere

into the screen, so to obtain a useful view of this we have rotated the sphere such that z is aligned vertically.

The final parameter of the Sphere command is the sweep angle. Rather than drawing the full 360° of the sphere you can choose to draw only part of it, rather like a slice of a pie. In Listing 8.2 we have specified a sweep angle of 270°, so Figure 8.2 shows only three-quarters of a full sphere. Note that this sweep is about the z axis.

Listing 8.2 The sweep angle of a sphere.

```
#sweep.rib
Display "sweep.tiff" "file" "rgba"
Projection "perspective"
WorldBegin
    Translate 0 0 4
    Sphere 2 -2 2 270
WorldEnd
```

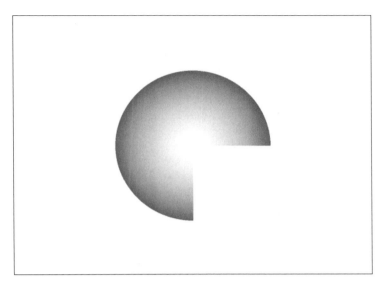

FIGURE 8.2. The sweep angle of a sphere

While `Sphere` is a somewhat limited modeling primitive, it demonstrates a number of important issues about the RenderMan API. The command describes what we want to be drawn, not how it should be drawn. In some other rendering APIs such as OpenGL you might have to provide a number of triangles or rectangles describing the sphere, or at least specify the level of detail with which it should be drawn. This leads to problems when you want to re-render a scene at a higher resolution, or use an extreme zoom on a simple model. The level of detail you have manually assigned for one image may not be appropriate in another.

While RenderMan does have commands to control the quality of the final image, the geometry we have passed to it is defined in a high level format. It is up to the renderer to decide how a sphere can best be rendered, and from the simple description it should be able to produce an image which appears perfectly smooth regardless of scale. While some renderers may choose to break the sphere into triangles, others may prefer to deal with the sphere as a single object. Regardless of how the renderer chooses to deal with geometry, this implementation detail should always be hidden from us.

Though not particularly flexible, `Sphere` and the other the primitives introduced in this chapter are very efficient to render and simple to texture, as we will see in Part 3. They also represent a perfectly smooth surface in an incredibly compact form, reducing RIB creation time and saving disk space. You should therefore use these simple surfaces in preference to more complex geometry when possible.

Cones and Cylinders

In addition to spheres you can create other simple geometric surfaces including cones and cylinders. Like spheres, these are always created at the origin and oriented about the *z*-axis, then transformed to the required location. In addition they all take a sweep angle, allowing only part of the object to be drawn.

To draw a cone you need to specify the height and the radius of the base followed by the sweep. For example, `Cone 2 0.5 360` draws a cone of height 2, and a base radius of 0.5. The cone is positioned so that the origin is at the centre of the base. A cylinder also requires a height and a radius. However, rather than specifying a height above the base, as in the case of a cone, a cylinder is allowed to extend both up and down the *z*-axis, and hence you must specify two distances. `Cylinder 0.5 -1 1 360` draws a cylinder two units high (−1 to 1 along the *z*-axis) and 1 unit in diameter (twice the radius of 0.5). These quadratic surfaces are shown in Figure 8.3, and the equivalent RIB is in Listing 8.3.

Listing 8.3 A cone and cylinder.

```
#coneCyl.rib
Display "coneCyl.tiff" "file" "rgba"

WorldBegin
Rotate -90 1 0 0
Translate 0 -8 0

TransformBegin
    Translate -3 0 -2
    Cone 5 2 360
TransformEnd

TransformBegin
    Translate 3 0 0
    Cylinder 2 -3 3 360
TransformEnd

WorldEnd
```

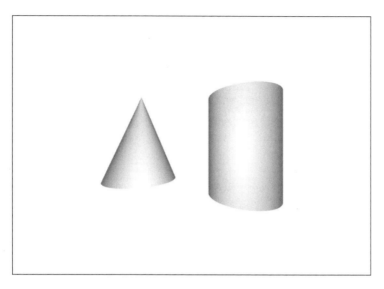

FIGURE 8.3. A cone and cylinder

The parameters to Cylinder and Cone are summarized in Figure 8.4.

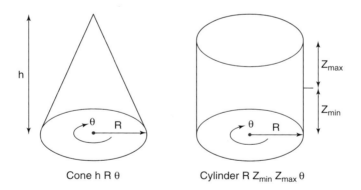

Cone h R θ Cylinder R Z_{min} Z_{max} θ

FIGURE 8.4. The cone and cylinder commands

Tori

The Torus command is slightly more complex as it draws a doughnut. This requires two radii—one known as the major radius from the centre of hole in the torus to the centre of the actual "dough," and the second minor radius defining the thickness of the "dough." These are followed by two sets of sweep angles as

shown in Figure 8.5. The minor sweep is specified first. It has the additional
control of having both a start and end angle.

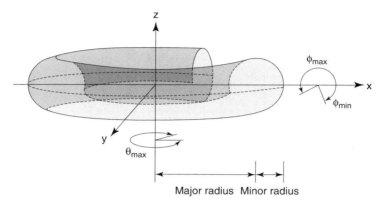

FIGURE 8.5. The torus command

Using only these simple primitives it is possible to construct relatively
complex scenes as seen in Figures 8.6 and 8.7. Once correctly shaded and
textured even the simplest geometry can produce visually interesting images.

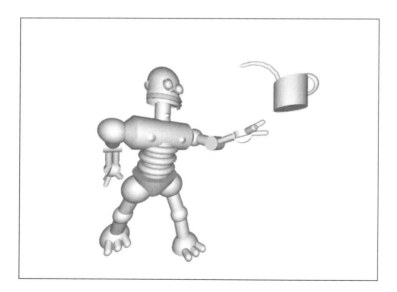

FIGURE 8.6. A robot created using only simple surfaces

FIGURE 8.7. Teddy bear

Summary

```
Sphere radius zmin zmax sweep ...
Cylinder radius zmin zmax sweep ...
Cone height radius sweep ...
Torus majrad minrad phimin phimax sweep ...
```

Related Commands

Disk height radius sweep

This command draws a disk around the *z*-axis of the specified radius. Unlike the other simple surfaces which are always centered at the origin the disk can be moved along the *z*-axis using the height parameter. This is useful for capping the end of cylinders which are otherwise open.

Paraboloid rmax zmin zmax sweep
Hyperboloid x1 y1 z1 x2 y2 z2 sweep

These commands draw two more complex geometric surfaces – the paraboloid and hyperboloid. A paraboloid is simply the 3D equivalent of the 2D parabola produced by the equation $y = x^2$ as shown in Figure 8.8. A hyperboloid is formed by rotating a line about the z-axis. This can be used to produce disks, cones, cylinders, lampshades and other more interesting shapes, as shown in Figure 8.9. Though the hyperboloid is based on a straight line the resulting shape is curved when the line is not parallel to the z-axis.

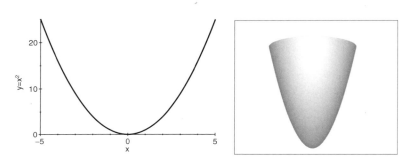

FIGURE 8.8. A parabola, and paraboloid

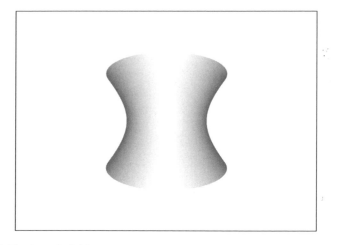

FIGURE 8.9. The hyperboloid

Chapter 9

Color and Other Attributes of Objects

Introduction

In addition to the geometry itself, we often need to specify properties of an object such as its color, which affect its appearance. In this chapter you will be introduced to the most common attributes, and learn how they can be managed.

Color

The objects we have drawn so far have all been white. However, we can easily specify that an object should be drawn in some other color by using the `Color` command. Though RenderMan supports more complex forms of color control, practically in all cases this is followed by three values enclosed in square brackets, specifying the amount of red, green, and blue required in the object. For example, if you want to make an object red you simply need to add the command: `Color [1 0 0]`. Like transforms, colors apply to everything that follows them, so the code in Listing 9.1 produces two red spheres. Of course this color is only a starting point for determining the color the object will appear in the rendered scene, as lighting and other shading effects must be taken into account, but in most cases `Color` is used as the basis of the final result.

Listing 9.1 Using color.

```
#red.rib
Display "red.tiff" "file" "rgba"
Projection "perspective"
WorldBegin
    #move everything back 2 units
    Translate 0 0 2
```

(Continued)

```
Color [ 1 0 0 ]

TransformBegin
      Translate −1 0 0
      Sphere 1 −1 1 360
TransformEnd

TransformBegin
      Translate 1 0 0
      Sphere 1 −1 1 360
TransformEnd
WorldEnd
```

Color is just one special case of an "attribute." Attributes are properties of objects which modify the way they are drawn.

Grouping Attributes

In the same way that you use TransformBegin/End to manage the scope of transforms, a similar pair of commands: AttributeBegin and AttributeEnd save and restore the current attributes. Using AttributeBegin/End allows us to draw an object, and be certain that it will have no effect on any other objects, as shown in Listing 9.2. This selects red as the current color, and then enters an Attribute block. Even though the color is changed to yellow in order to draw the left-hand sphere, the previous color (red) is restored upon exit from the Attribute block, so the right sphere appears red in Figure 9.1.

Listing 9.2 Controlling the scope of attributes.

```
Display "beginend.tiff" "file" "rgba"
Projection "perspective"
WorldBegin
Translate 0 0 2

Color [ 1 0 0 ]

AttributeBegin
      Translate −1 0 0
      Color [ 1 1 0 ]
      Sphere 1 −1 1 360
AttributeEnd
#This resets the color back to red

AttributeBegin
      Translate 1 0 0
      Sphere 1 −1 1 360
AttributeEnd

WorldEnd
```

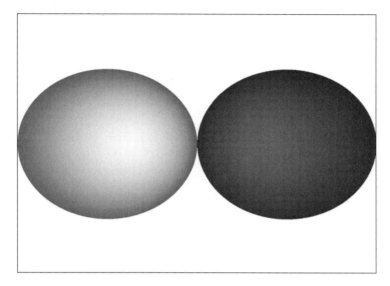

Controlling the scope of attributes

Transformations are a special case of attributes, so `AttributeBegin` performs the action of `TransformBegin` implicitly, and similarly for `AttributeEnd`.

Opacity

A second important attribute is opacity. In the same way that the `Color` command allows you to specify how light is reflected from the surface, you can use `Opacity` to specify how light is transmitted though the surface. When light is shone at a surface from the front, the light reflected back depends on the color of the light and the color of the surface. When a light is shone through a surface from behind, then the color of the light seen through the surface depends on the color of the light and the opacity of the surface. Opacity is therefore also specified as a color. For example in Listing 9.3 we have asked the renderer to draw two spheres, which overlap each other. The green sphere has a transparency of `[0.5 0.5 0.5]`—that is, it lets half of the red light through, half the green and half the blue—hence you can see the red sphere inside the green one in Figure 9.2.

The opacity of a surface can potentially be very different to its color. For example, stained glass is highly colored when viewer in transmitted light (opacity), yet appears very dull or even black when viewed in reflected light (color).You might set the color and opacity of red glass to `[ 0.1 0.1 0.1 ]` and `[ 1 0 0 ]`, respectively.

Listing 9.3 Opacity.

```
Display "opacity.tiff" "file" "rgba"
Projection "perspective"
WorldBegin
#move everything back 2 units
Translate 0 0 2

Color [ 1 0 0 ]

AttributeBegin
    Translate -0.25 0 0
    Color [ 0 1 0 ]
    Opacity [ 0.5 0.5 0.5 ]
    Sphere 1 -1 1 360
AttributeEnd

AttributeBegin
    Translate 0.25 0 0
    Sphere 1 -1 1 360
AttributeEnd

WorldEnd
```

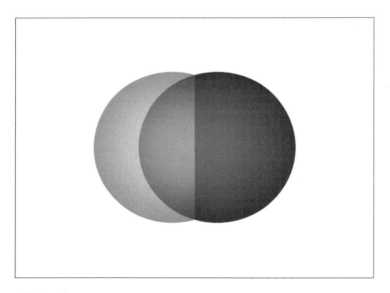

FIGURE 9.2. Opacity

Other Attributes

ShadingRate

Calculation of position and final color is performed at multiple points on the surface of each object. The number of points required for each object is automatically calculated by the renderer, but under certain circumstances you might want to modify the default value. This is controlled through the command ShadingRate. The default shading rate of 1.0 should be adequate in most cases, but a higher value (ShadingRate 3.0) allows you to trade quality for reduced render times. A lower value (ShadingRate 0.4) forces the renderer to use more points on the surface which may in some cases improve the quality of the final image. The effect of increasing shading rate is shown in Listing 9.4 and Figure 9.3—note how the shading becomes less smooth and more blocky as the shading rate is increased from left to right.

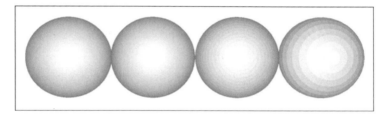

FIGURE 9.3. Changing the shading rate

Listing 9.4 Changing the shading rate.

```
Display "shading.tiff" "file" "rgba"
WorldBegin

Translate 0 0 6

ShadingRate 1
Translate -1.5 0 0
Sphere 0.5 -0.5 0.5 360

ShadingRate 2
Translate 1 0 0
Sphere 0.5 -0.5 0.5 360
```

(Continued)

```
ShadingRate 4
Translate 1 0 0
Sphere 0.5 -0.5 0.5 360

ShadingRate 8
Translate 1 0 0
Sphere 0.5 -0.5 0.5 360
WorldEnd
```

Matte

When computer graphics are combined live action, a proxy object is sometimes placed in the CG scene to represent a real world object which will later be composited into place. This object should not appear in the final render, but will still obscure objects behind it. Such an object is known as a matte, and hence this property is specified by the `Matte` attribute. `Matte  1` indicates that the object should be treated in this special way, while `Matte   0` specifies a regularly rendered object.

Shaders

The shaders applied to an object to describe its surface characteristics are also attributes but these are of sufficient complexity and importance that they deserve a chapter in their own right.

Summary

```
AttributeBegin
AttributeEnd
Color [r g b]
Opacity [r g b]
Matte bool
ShadingRate size
```

Related Commands

Sides n
Orientation "handedness"
ReverseOrientation

When you render an object it usually has a front and back, but provided the object is opaque, from any single point of view you can only see the front. Even though it seems obvious, you can not see the back of objects, the renderer may have to do a lot of work to figure that out for itself. You may be able to reduce render time by giving the renderer a hint that it only need draw half the object. If the `Sides` attribute is set to 1 then the renderer will immediately throw away the back of objects.

For various reasons the renderer may inadvertently throw away the wrong side–removing the front rather than the back. You can control this by passing "inside" or "outside" to the `Orientation` command. `ReverseOrientation` tells it to draw the other side to the one it would normally draw.

Attribute *"attributeType"* *"name"* [*val*]

Though Pixar included many possible attributes in RenderMan standard, they also included a mechanism for developers of renderers to add their own using the `Attribute` command. These are typically arranged in groups, sharing a common first parameter, and then a more specific attribute name as the second. The value of the parameter follows in square brackets. Refer to your renderer's documentation to find out what custom attributes it supports.

Chapter 10
Camera Setup

Introduction

A renderer is much like a camera in that it turns a three-dimensional scene into a two-dimensional image. Just as a real camera has many controls that affect exactly how the image should be recorded, so the renderer can record the same scene in a range of different ways. In this section, we will examine some of the options available for controlling the final image.

Options

Attributes control parameters that are specified on a per-object basis. In addition to these, some parameters apply to the whole image. These can be considered as defining the virtual camera that is being used to view the scene, and are known as "options." As options apply to the whole scene they cannot be changed while a frame is being rendered. You can't place option commands between `World-Begin` and `WorldEnd`. We have already used two options: `Display` and `Projection`, which control where the rendered image is to be stored, and how three-dimensional space is to be reduced down to two dimensions.

Field of View

You may have noticed that many of the images produced so far appear distorted at the edges of the frame. This is an artifact of the projection being used, and the large field of view. By default an image rendered using the perspective projection is rendered with a 90-degree field of view (Figure 10.1). As RenderMan measures

FOV based on the shortest side of the image (typically the height), this corresponds to an ultra-wide-angle—equivalent to a 12 mm lens on a 35 mm film camera. You can reduce this distortion by moving the objects further away from the camera and then reducing the field of view to simulate zooming in with a telephoto lens as shown in Figure 10.2. Field of view is specified by passing a "fov" parameter to the perspective projection in Listing 10.1.

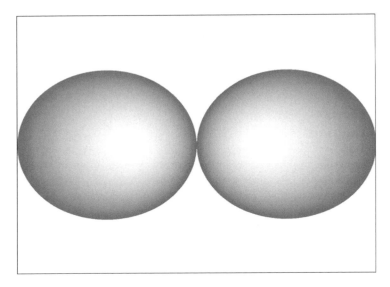

FIGURE 10.1. Field of view = 90°

Listing 10.1 Field of view = 20.

```
Display "fovfar.tiff" "file" "rgba"
Projection "perspective" "fov" [ 20 ]
WorldBegin
    Translate 0 0 10
    TransformBegin
        Translate -1 0 0
        Sphere 1 -1 1 360
    TransformEnd
    TransformBegin
        Translate 1 0 0
        Sphere 1 -1 1 360
    TransformEnd
WorldEnd
```

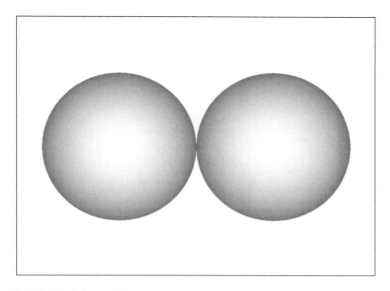

Figure 10.2. Field of view = 20°

In the following chapters we will use this mechanism of passing parameters by specifying their name followed by one or more values enclosed in square brackets with many other commands.

Positioning the Camera

As the camera is the only fixed point of reference in our scene, it can not be moved as such but we can produce the same effect by moving all of the objects in the world. We have done this previously by placing transforms within the WorldBegin/End block. However, by placing transforms after the Projection command and before the WorldBegin command you can explicitly transform the whole world. The position of the world is specified in terms of the camera, objects are specified in terms of the world, and hence this effectively moves the camera.

At present it will have no effect upon your images whether you place transforms inside or outside of the world block, and merely serves as a useful convention to distinguish camera movement from object movement. However, the ability to distinguish the position of an object relative to a static world even when the camera is moving will become more important when we start to shade our objects in Part 3.

This is demonstrated in Listing 10.2.

Listing 10.2 Setting options.

```
#exposure.rib
Display "exposure.tiff" "file" "rgba"
Format 640 480 1.0
Clipping 5 15
PixelSamples 2 2
Exposure 1.0 2.2
Projection "perspective" "fov" [25]
Translate 0 0 10
WorldBegin
    Sphere 2 -2 2 360
WorldEnd
```

Clipping

When a scene is rendered, the renderer will try and discard any objects which are too close or too far away from the camera. Those too far away are redundant because they simply would not be visible, while objects close to the camera are difficult to render, and probably off-screen anyway. However, the renderer needs some hints as to what should be considered too close or too far away. You can give the renderer this information using the Clipping command and its two parameters, *hither* and *yon*.

Any part of an object closer than *hither* will be removed, as will those past *yon*. *Hither* in particular is worth paying attention to if any geometry is close to the camera, as by increasing its value only slightly you can dramatically improve render times. When correctly set this option should not affect the rendered image.

The Clipping command is used in Listing 10.2, where the sphere is positioned 10 units back. Anything closer than 5 or further than 15 units is discarded.

Image Resolution

We have so far been rendering our images at 640 pixels wide by 480 pixels high, as this is the default output resolution. However, you can control the resolution of the final image by using the Format command. This takes a height and width for the output image measured in pixels.

The third parameter to Format specifies the pixel aspect ratio. Most computer displays have square pixels—an image 100 by 100 pixels would appear square on screen, but this is not the case for video formats which tend to squash the image slightly. If your image is to be displayed on such a device then you need to make sure this squash is taken into account during rendering by setting the pixel aspect ratio appropriately. A frame for output on PAL video might therefore contain the line `Format 768 576 0.9`. More immediately you might want to reduce the size of the output image in order to speed up test renders using `Format 320 240 1.0`.

Super Sampling

Though `Format` specifies how many pixels the render needs to output, internally it will calculate the color at many more points for each output pixel, averaging them together to produce the final pixel color. This "super sampling" reduces rendering artifacts, and produces a higher quality image, at the cost of additional render time. You can control the number of points calculated per pixel by using the `PixelSamples` command. A setting of `PixelSamples 1 1` will render quickly using only one sample per pixel, while a setting of `PixelSamples 4 4` will evaluate 16 samples per pixels, roughly arranged in a 4 by 4 grid.

Exactly how many samples you need to use depends on the contents of your image, and what you intend to use it for. Consider Figure 10.3 which consists of three images rendered with increasing samples. The first image is clearly blocky at the edges of the sphere, while the second is a distinct improvement. The third image is marginally better but for this simple image the effect is not particularly marked. When we start experimenting with advanced techniques such as depth of field and motion blur you will probably need to increase the number of samples used to avoid artifacts.

Listing 10.2 explicitly sets the output resolution and super sampling to their default values of 640 480, and 2 2.

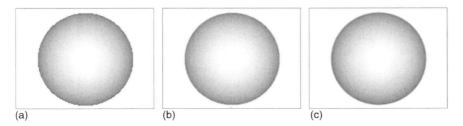

(a)   (b)   (c)

FIGURE 10.3. Pixel Samples (**a**) 1 1 (**b**) 2 2 (**c**) 4 4

Exposure

Having finally calculated the correct color of each pixel, we needs to display the resultant image. Unfortunately such things are rarely simple. The value calculated by the renderer is "linear"—that is a pixel with a brightness of 0.8 should appear twice as bright as a pixel with a brightness of 0.4. While you probably consider this a perfectly normal situation, it is not the result that is obtained when an image is sent to a typical video device. Most devices have a nonlinear response, which would result in the 0.4 pixel being much darker than it should be. This nonlinearity is known as gamma, and can be summarized for individual devices, or more generally for a type of device by a single number. A gamma value of one would represent a linear device, while most computer screens have a value in the range 1.5—2.0. Some official standards for video screens specify a gamma value of 2.2, but this is not particularly reliable.

When previewing images it is important that you use imaging software which corrects the gamma of the image being displayed to match the display on which it is being viewed. However, when you are rendering the final results, which will then be transferred to a specific output device such as video tape, a higher quality image can be produced by gamma correcting in the renderer. You can do this by using the `Exposure` command (Listing 10.2), which takes two parameters – `gain` and `gamma`. `Gain` is simply a multiplier which makes the image brighter or darker. `Gamma` controls the contrast, and generates a nonlinear image. Figure 10.4 is rendered with a gamma of 2.2, resulting in the edges of the sphere which have previously been very dark, appearing much lighter.

FIGURE 10.4. Increasing gamma

If your output device requires a gamma correction of 2.2 then including the command `Exposure 1.0 2.2` will produce an image with a better balance between the light and dark areas *when viewed on the target output device*. Viewing on a linear device would make it appear washed out. You should only use this approach when the image generated is being sent directly to the output device, as any compositing or color correction that may be done post-render cannot be applied to nonlinear images. In such cases it would be more appropriate to output linear images, which can be gamma corrected after they have been processed.

Summary

```
Projection "projectionname" "fov" [angle ]
Clipping hither yon
Format xres yres pixelaspect
PixelSamples x y
Exposure gain gamma
```

Related Commands

PixelFilter "filtername" xwidth ywidth

While it may appear counterintuitive, simply adding together all the samples generated for a pixel does not produce the best possible final image. For reasons that are somewhat complex, a higher quality image can be produced by weighting the samples such that samples near the centre of the pixels are considered more important. Samples from outside the pixel's boundary should also be included, some samples even being subtracted rather than added. The method used to calculate the average pixel color is controlled by the `PixelFilter` command.

Quantize Scale min max dither

By default most renderers will produce an eight bits per channel image, with black being stored as zero, and white being stored as 255. The `Quantize` command allows images to be stored at a higher level of detail such as 16 bit or floating point format, and gives some control over how brightness levels are represented.

Option "OptionType" "name" [val]

Just as the `Attribute` command allows renderers to define new properties of objects, so the Option command allows additional camera controls not originally included in the RenderMan API to be specified.

Chapter 11
Lighting

Introduction

A well-constructed scene consists of more than just objects and a camera. The positioning and control of lighting is an essential aspect, whether you are attempting to create a realistic, theatrical, or cinematic look. In this chapter, we will look at the various types of light that are available in RenderMan, and see how you can use these in a RIB file. These will allow you to illuminate your scene in a more interesting fashion than the default lighting we have so far been using.

A Plastic Object

All the objects we have created so far have had a simple lighting model applied to them—surfaces directly facing the camera are bright, while those at an acute angle appear darker. This default model gives an adequate sense of shape and has allowed us to create basic scenes, but for greater realism we need surfaces which can react to light in more interesting ways.

One of the most powerful features of a RenderMan renderer is support for shaders. These allow the appearance of an object to be controlled in almost any way imaginable. We will consider shaders in the following chapter, but more immediately we need something which can be lit by the lights we are about to create. The shader "plastic," which produces the standard computer-generated look, is perfect for this. You simply need to include the line `Surface "plastic"` in the RIB file and any object that follows will be made out of plastic.

Upon attaching the plastic shader and rendering the scene you should be rewarded with a totally black image. The default surface is self-illuminating, but most shaders including plastic require some kind of lighting—as in real life without any lights, a plastic object will simply appear black.

Pointlight

You can create a light by using the `LightSource` command. Like surfaces, lights are controlled by shaders, but several standard lights are available. The "`pointlight`" shader creates a light that shines equally in all directions, rather like a naked light bulb. By default it is centered at the origin, but we can move it around using the standard transform commands. Alternativly, we can place the light using a "`from`" parameter, as in Listing 11.1. Parameter lists of this kind can be applied to many commands—we used them previously to specify the field of view of the camera—and take the form of a parameter name followed by an array of values enclosed in square brackets. Fortunately, parameters always have default values so we can ignore any parameters that we are not interested in.

Listing 11.1 Pointlight.

```
#pointlight.rib
Display "pointlight.tiff" "file" "rgba"
Format 640 480 1.0

Projection "perspective" "fov" [ 30 ]

Translate 0 0 5

WorldBegin
    LightSource "pointlight" 1
        "from" [ -2 2 -2]
        "intensity" [ 7 ]
    Surface "plastic"
    Color [ 1 0 0 ]
    Sphere 1 -1 1 360
WorldEnd
```

For a "`pointlight`" the only parameter other than "from" you will regularly need to modify is "`intensity`." When first placed in a scene the pointlight source often appears dim because it is defined to obey an inverse square law—for each doubling of the distance from the light the intensity drops by a factor of four. This is exactly how lights behave in the real world, but many other renderers use a different lighting model, as nonphysically based lights can make it easier to light scenes in an aesthetically pleasing (though less realistic) fashion. It is very simple to create nonphysically accurate lights in RenderMan, but for now you need simply note that intensity will probably have a value greater than one, as it will be attenuated by the distance from light to surface.

The result of illuminating a red plastic sphere with a point light source is shown in Figure 11.1 (also Plate I).

FIGURE 11.1. Pointlight (also Plate I)

The number following the shader name is a light source "handle" – simply a unique number you can use to refer to the light. This allows you to create lights at the beginning of a scene, and then apply them only to certain objects, giving greater control. As an alternative to using a number to identify a particular light source, most modern implementations of RenderMan will also allow you to give the light a name. Simply use a string as the handle (for example, "myLight") in place of the number.

The `Illuminate` command is used to turn lights on and off, and takes two parameters: a light handle followed by 1 for on or 0 for off. This is shown in Listing 11.2 (also Plate I) where one light source and two spheres are created, but `Illuminate` is used to turn off the light source for the right sphere. As a result in Figure 11.2 only the left sphere is lit, while the other remains black.

Listing 11.2 Turning a light off and on.

```
#illuminate.rib
Display "illuminate.tiff" "file" "rgba"
Projection "perspective" "fov" [20]
Translate 0 0 10

WorldBegin
    LightSource
        "pointlight" "myLight"
        "from" [3 3 -5]
        "intensity" [25]
```

(*Continued*)

```
    Surface "plastic"
    Color [ 1 0 0 ]

AttributeBegin
    Illuminate "myLight" 1
    Translate -0.5 0 0
    Sphere 1 -1 1 360
AttributeEnd

AttributeBegin
    Illuminate "myLight" 0
    Translate 0.5 0 0
    Sphere 1 -1 1 360
AttributeEnd

WorldEnd
```

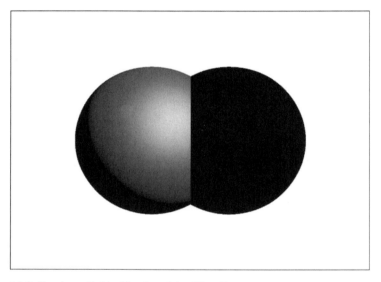

FIGURE 11.2. Turning a light off and on (also Plate I)

The state of a light source is an attribute, and hence it is possible to save and restore the currently active lights using AttributeBegin/End.

Distantlights

While the point light has a position, but no orientation, certain light sources have an orientation, but effectively no position. These are known as "distantlights" and are typically used to represent daylight. The illumination of an object lit by the sun changes little as the object moves within the scene (excluding shadows). However, illumination is highly dependent on the object's orientation—is it facing towards the sun or away from it?

To create a "distantlight" you therefore need to specify a "to" parameter that describes the direction in which the light is shining. Listing 11.3 creates a light shining to the right, the results of which can be seen in Figure 11.3 (also Plate I).

Listing 11.3 Distantlight.

```
#distantlight.rib
Display "distantlight.tiff" "file" "rgba"

Projection "perspective" "fov" [ 30 ]

Translate 0 0 5

WorldBegin
    LightSource "distantlight" 1
        "to" [ 1 0 0 ]
        "intensity" [ 1 ]

    Color [ 1 0 0 ]
    Surface "plastic"
    Sphere 1 -1 1 360
WorldEnd
```

FIGURE 11.3. Distantlight (also Plate I)

Spotlights

Just as in cinema or theatre, when maximum control over the lighting of scene is required, you should use some form of spotlight. The standard "spotlight" shader provided with all RenderMan implementations behaves like a standard theatrical spotlight and hence has both a position and an orientation, specified using a "from" and a "to" parameter.

The "from" of a spotlight specifies its postion, while "to" specifies a point towards which the spot is shining. In Listing 11.4 we have created a spotlight, illuminating a plastic sphere. By specifying "to" as [0 0 0] the spotlight points towards the centre of the sphere. A spotlight produces a circular beam as shown in Figure 11.4 (also Plate I).

Listing 11.4 Spotlight.

```
#spotlight.rib
Display "spotlight.tiff" "file" "rgba"
Projection "perspective" "fov" [ 30 ]

Translate 0 0 5

WorldBegin
    LightSource "spotlight" 2
        "from" [-2 2 -2]
        "to" [ 0 0 0 ]
        "intensity" [ 7 ]
        "coneangle" [0.25]
        "conedeltaangle" [0.05]

    Color [ 1 0 0 ]
    Surface "plastic"
    Sphere 1 -1 1 360
WorldEnd
```

FIGURE 11.4. Spotlight (also Plate I)

A spotlight also allows you to control exactly how directional the light is using the "`coneangle`" and "`deltaangle`" parameters, illustrated in Figure 11.5. Outside the "`coneangle`" (specified in radians) the light has no effect, while within `coneangle-deltaangle` the full intensity of the light is in effect. Between these two angles the light falls-off smoothly producing a soft edge to the beam. This can be seen in Figure 11.6 (also Plate I) where the delta angle (specified in Listing 11.5) has been increased to produce a softer edge to the light.

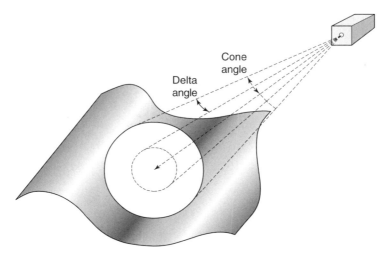

FIGURE 11.5. Cone angle and delta angle

Listing 11.5 Softening the edge of a spot.

```
#delta.rib
Display "delta.tiff" "file" "rgba"
Projection "perspective" "fov" [ 30 ]

Translate 0 0 5

WorldBegin
    LightSource "spotlight" 2
        "from" [-2 2 -2]
        "to" [ 0 0 0 ]
        "intensity" [ 7 ]
        "coneangle" [0.25]
        "conedeltaangle" [0.25]
    Color [ 1 0 0 ]
    Surface "plastic"
    Sphere 1 -1 1 360
WorldEnd
```

FIGURE 11.6. Softening the edge of a spotlight (also Plate I)

Ambient Lights

In the real world, each light source would emit light into the scene which would then bounce from surfaces, and illuminate other surfaces which are not directly lit. In computer graphics this is known as global illumination and is modeled using techniques like photon mapping. While we will consider global illumination in a later chapter, all methods of global illumination are slow, and, therefore, must be used sparingly. In many cases, you can fake this indirect illumination by simply adding a little extra light to each surface using an "ambientlight" source.

An ambient light as defined in Listing 11.6, illuminates all surfaces equally regardless of their position or orientation. A consequence of this is that, it removes clues as to the depth of the scene. This can be seen in the resultant image in Figure 11.7 (also Plate I) which is totally flat. However, if you use an

Listing 11.6 Ambientlight.

```
#ambientlight.rib
Display "ambientlight.tiff" "file" "rgba"
Projection "perspective" "fov" [ 30 ]

Translate 0 0 5

WorldBegin
    LightSource "ambientlight" 1
        "intensity" [ 0.5 ]

    Color [ 1 0 0 ]
    Surface "plastic"
    Sphere 1 -1 1 360
WorldEnd
```

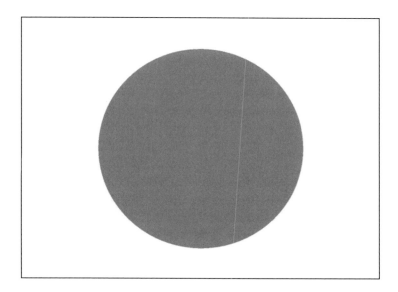

FIGURE 11.7. Ambientlight (also Plate I)

"ambientlight" in combination with other lights, adding as little as possible
to avoid areas of total black, it can soften your lighting and produce a better
image. Listing 11.7 takes this approach to produce the image in Figure 11.8
(also Plate I).

Listing 11.7 Ambient and spotlight.

```
#spotambient.rib
Display "spotambient.tiff" "file" "rgba"
Projection "perspective" "fov" [ 30 ]

Translate 0 0 5

WorldBegin
    LightSource "ambientlight" 1
        "intensity" [ 0.1]
    LightSource "spotlight" 2
        "from" [-2 2 -2]
        "to" [ 0 0 0 ]
        "intensity" [ 7 ]
        "coneangle" [0.25]
        "conedeltaangle" [0.05]

    Color [ 1 0 0 ]
    Surface "plastic"
    Sphere 1 -1 1 360
WorldEnd
```

FIGURE 11.8. Ambient and spotlight (also Plate I)

Many renderers support other lights in addition to the standard ones. Uberlight, for example, provides a much greater degree of control than any of the standard lights, including options for avoiding many of the inconveniences of physics. Details of any additional light types will be provided in the documentation for your renderer.

Summary

```
Surface "shadername" ...
LightSource "shadername" handle ...
Illuminate handle bool
LightSource "pointlight" 1
        "from" [ x y z ]
        "intensity" [ val ]
        "lightcolor" [ r g b ]
LightSource "distantlight" 2
        "to" [ x y z ]
        "intensity" [ val ]
        "lightcolor" [ r g b ]
LightSource "spotlight" 3
        "from" [ x y z ]
        "to" [ x y z ]
        "intensity" [ val ]
        "lightcolor" [ r g b ]
        "coneangle" [ angle ]
        "conedeltaangle" [angle]
LightSource "ambientlight" 4
        "intensity" [ val ]
        "lightcolor" [ r g b ]
```

Chapter 12
The Standard Surface Types

Introduction

Having set up some lights, we can now consider how those lights interact with the surfaces in our scene. This interaction is controlled by a surface shader. Shaders are one of the most important aspects of RenderMan, to such an extent that the second half of this book will be totally dedicated to creating new shaders. However, before we consider how you can write your own shaders we will first examine the standard shaders that are defined by the RenderMan standard and are available by default in all renderers.

Shaders are attatched to objects using the `Surface` command followed by the name of the shader to be used. They are attributes, as they are are applied on a per object basis, and hence can be stored and recalled by `AttributeBegin` and `AttributeEnd`.

Constant

The simplest surface is "`constant`." Even simpler than the default surface we have used earlier, the constant shader simply takes the color defined in the RIB and uses it as the output color, ignoring all lighting in the scene. Naturally, this results in a totally flat appearance, as in Figure 12.1 (also Plate II), and is of limited use when generating photorealistic images. You might choose to use it, however, to produce images that are deliberately stylized, or for images that are going to be postprocessed.

Listing 12.1 shows the basic RIB file used in this chapter. A spotlight is used to provide the key light of the scene, while an ambient is used to fill in the dark side. The shader—in this case "`constant`"—is attached to a sphere using the command `Surface`. To better illustrate the shaders appearance we have also displayed it on a more complex object.

FIGURE 12.1. The "constant" shader (also Plate II)

Listing 12.1 The "constant" shader.

```
#constant.rib
Display "constant.tiff" "file" "rgba"
Projection "perspective" "fov" [ 30 ]

Translate 0 0 5

WorldBegin
    LightSource "ambientlight" 1 "intensity" [ 0.1 ]
    LightSource "spotlight" 2
        "from" [-2 2 -2]
        "to" [ 0 0 0 ]
        "intensity" [ 7 ]
        "coneangle" [0.25]
        "conedeltaangle" [0.05]

    Color [ 1 0 0 ]
    Surface "constant"
    Sphere 1 -1 1 360
WorldEnd
```

Matte

For most applications, we require something which takes into account the lighting of the scene, and the position of the surface to give an appearance of depth. This can be achieved using the surface shader "matte," as shown in Figure 12.2 (also Plate II). This simulates the diffuse scattering of light from a rough surface (such as a brown envelope). When light in the scene hits a matte object it is scattered in all directions. As a result the color of the surface as it appears when rendered is independent of where you place the camera.

FIGURE 12.2. The "matte" shader (also Plate II)

As with most of the other surface shaders, "matte" also responds to ambient light that has no direction. The amount of ambient and diffuse light scattered by the matte surface can be scaled using the parameters "Ka" and "Kd," respectively. For example, to create surfaces which are unaffected by ambient light we could use the command Surface "matte" "Ka" [0]. The matte shader should not be confused with the Matte attribute command. The two are totally unrelated and the unfortunate clash of names is purely coincidental.

Metal

Metallic objects are usually identifiable by the way they reflect bright light, creating a sharp specular highlight. In contrast to the "matte" shader, the location of this bright spot on the surface is highly dependent on the position of the observer. Light hitting a metallic surface is reflected as if in a mirror, and only when viewed from near the mirror angle will the highlight be visible.

Of course not all metal surfaces are as highly polished, and in these cases, the light will be scattered in a cone around the mirror angle, the size of which depends on the roughness of the surface—a rough surface will produce a less sharply defined highlight, while a smooth surface would produce a small and sharp bright point.

You can simulate these effects by use of the "metal" shader which is illustrated in Figure 12.3 (also Plate II). The brightness of the highlight can be controlled by the "Ks" parameter, while the size of the highlight is set by the "roughness" parameter (Figure 12.4 and Plate III).

FIGURE 12.3. The "metal" shader (also Plate II)

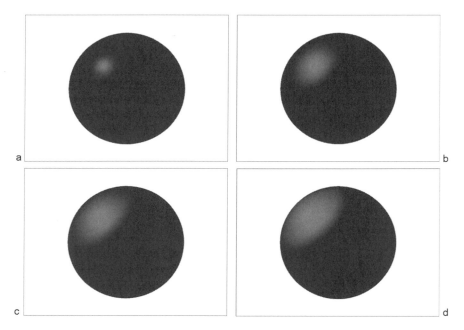

FIGURE 12.4. (**a**) roughness = 0.01 (**b**) roughness = 0.05 (**c**) roughness = 0.1 (**d**) roughness = 0.2 (also Plate III)

Plastic

If you examine a plastic surface, you should be able to observe that such materials generally combine both a diffuse and a specular component. Colored plastic is manufactured by suspending particles of color inside a clear "glue." Light can either be reflected in a specular fashion from the smooth surface of the glue producing a white highlight, or scattered randomly from the colored particles like a matte surface. The "`plastic`" shader shown in Figure 12.5 (also Plate II) therefore has the properties and parameters of both "`matte`" and "`metal`." In addition, it allows the color of the specular highlight to be controlled by the parameter "`specularcolor`".

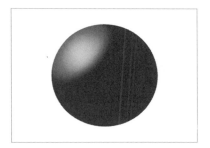 

FIGURE 12.5. The "`plastic`" shader (also Plate II)

When you create a metal surface, it is likely that you will find the standard metal shader difficult to control. Its lack of a diffuse component results in surfaces that are difficult to light evenly. In such cases you can create a metallic appearance using the plastic shader by setting "`specularcolor`" to be the same as the standard RIB color. For example:

```
Color [ 1 0 0 ]
Surface "plastic" "Kd" [0.1] "Ks" [0.9]
                  "specularcolor" [ 1 0 0 ]
```

Setting Ks to 1 and Kd to 0, would produce results identical to the metal shader, but by slightly increasing Kd (and reducing Ks), you can fill in some of the dark areas of the surface without relying too heavily on ambient light. This is demonstrated in Figure 12.6 (also Plate III) which uses the plastic shader to create a more controlled metallic appearance.

FIGURE 12.6. Using "`plastic`" to stimulate metal (also Plate III)

Painted Plastic

The most complex standard shader, "`paintedplastic`", extends plastic by
allowing a texture map to be used to control the base color, rather than the uniform
RIB color. The name of the image file is passed to the shader using the parameter
"`texturename`," as in Listing 12.2. If you were to apply the texture file shown
in Figure 12.7, the resultant image would be Figure 12.8 (also Plate III).

Listing 12.2 The "paintedplastic" shader.

```
#painted.rib
Display "painted.tiff" "file" "rgba"
Projection "perspective" "fov" [ 30 ]

Translate 0 0 5

WorldBegin
    LightSource "ambientlight" 1 "intensity" [ 0.1 ]
    LightSource "spotlight" 2
        "from" [-2 2 -2]
        "to" [ 0 0 0 ]
        "intensity" [ 7 ]
        "coneangle" [0.25]
        "conedeltaangle" [0.05]
```

```
    Color [ 1 0 0 ]
    Surface "paintedplastic"
        "texturename" ["swirl.tiff"]
    Rotate 90 1 0 0
    Sphere 1 -1 1 360
WorldEnd
```

FIGURE 12.7. A sample texture

FIGURE 12.8. The "paintedplastic" shader (also Plate III)

The format of the image file is dependent upon the renderer, and while many renderers will accept the TIFF file format, in most cases you can increase rendering speeds by using a format specific to the renderer. These formats are optimized for texture lookup, and can dramatically reduce memory requirements when rendering images with large textures. For PRMan the command to generate these optimized image files is txmake—running the command "txmake image.tiff image.tx" creates a new texture file "image.tx," optimized for PRMan's use. Other renderers will have their own texture formatting tools, described in their documentation.

Summary

```
Surface "constant"
Surface "matte""Ka" [ 1 ]
    "Kd" [ 1 ]
Surface "metal""Ka" [ 1 ]
    "Ks" [ 1 ]
    "roughness" [0.1]
Surface "plastic"
    "Ka" [ 1 ]
    "Kd" [ 0.5 ]
    "Ks" [ 0.5 ]
    "roughness" [ 0.1 ]
    "specularcolor" [ 1 1 1 ]
Surface "paintedplastic"
    "Ka" [ 1 ]
    "Kd" [ 0.5 ]
    "Ks" [ 0.5 ]
    "roughness" [0.1]
    "specularcolor" [ 1 1 1 ]
    "texturename" [ "" ]
```

Related Commands

Displacement "name" . . .

Surface shaders are used to control the surface color of an object but
RenderMan supports many other types of shaders that you can use to control
other aspects of the rendering process. One shader of each type may be attached
to an object.

A displacement shader, specified with the `Displacement` command
(Listing 12.3) allows you to deform a surface, adding creases, bumps, scratches,
or other fine details which would be difficult to produce using geometry. Such
a shader is demonstrated in Figure 12.9 (also Plate III). Note that the displacement
shader is specified in addition to a surface shader—the surface is still made
of plastic even though it has been displaced. Though there are no standard
displacement shaders, many renderers ship with a number of displacement
shaders such as "dented."

Listing 12.3 A displacement shader.

```
#dented.rib
Display "dented.tiff" "file" "rgba"
Projection "perspective" "fov" [ 30 ]

Translate 0 0 5

WorldBegin
    LightSource "ambientlight" 1 "intensity" [ 0.1 ]
    LightSource "spotlight" 2
        "from" [-2 2 -2]
        "to" [ 0 0 0 ]
        "intensity" [ 7 ]
        "coneangle" [0.25]
        "conedeltaangle" [0.05]

    Color [ 1 0 0 ]
    Surface "plastic"
    Displacement "dented"
    Sphere 1 -1 1 360
WorldEnd
```

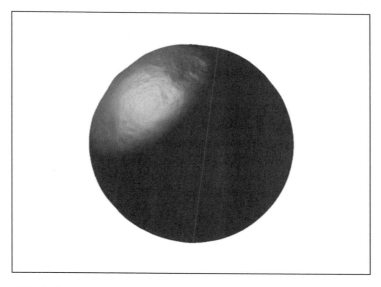

FIGURE 12.9. A displacement shader (also Plate III)

Chapter 13
More Complex Surfaces

Introduction

While objects like spheres and cones have allowed us to create elegant geometry from a small number of simple commands, we clearly need more flexible surfaces that will allow us to model a wider range of shapes. In this chapter, we will introduce a number of surface types that allow you to create almost any form of object.

Polygons

Though it has a number of limitations, the easiest method of constructing a surface is to approximate it using a number of flat polygons. This allows you to produce any shape to any required level of detail. In fact many non-RenderMan renderers use polygons as their only form of geometry.

You can generate polygons in RenderMan by using the `Polygon` command, which draws a single polygon. The corners of this polygon are specified as points in counter-clockwise order by a parameter "P." For example, the command shown in Listing 13.1 draws a unit square in the *xy* plane, as can be seen in Figure 13.1. This polygon has four corners, but any number may be used provided that they are coplaner—that is, the polygon must be flat.

Listing 13.1 A simple polygon.

```
#polygon.rib
Display "polygon.tiff" "file" "rgba"
Projection "perspective" "fov" [ 30 ]

Translate -0.5 -0.5 3

WorldBegin
    LightSource "ambientlight" 1 "intensity" [ 0.1 ]
```

(Continued)

```
    LightSource "pointlight" 2
              "from" [-2 2 -2]
              "intensity" [ 7 ]
    Color [ 1 0 0 ]
    Surface "plastic"
    Polygon "P" [ 0 0 0
                  1 0 0
                  1 1 0
                  0 1 0 ]
WorldEnd
```

FIGURE 13.1. A simple polygon

General Polygons

The `Polygon` command also has the restriction that the polygon must be convex: if you draw a line from any point in the polygon to any other point in the polygon, that line is not allowed to cross any of the edges of the polygon. To render concave polygons you must use the command `GeneralPolygon`. This is slightly more complex to use, as it also allows you to cut holes into the polygon. Despite the relaxing of other restrictions general polygons must still be planer.

A general polygon is made from one or more "loops," each of which may contain any number of points. The first loop defines the boundary of the polygon, while subsequent loops cut holes into it. To define a `GeneralPolygon` you must first tell the renderer how many points comprise each loop, and then provide an array containing all of the points, for each loop in turn. For example, in Listing 13.2 the `GeneralPolygon` command is followed by an array with two elements: 4 and 3 indicating that the polygon to be drawn is a quadrilateral (actually a square) with a triangle cut out from it. The first four points of the "P" parameter define the square, and the next three define the triangle, as shown in Figure 13.2.

Listing 13.2 A general polygon.

```
#general.rib
Display "general.tiff" "file" "rgba"
Projection "perspective" "fov" [ 30 ]

Translate -0.5 -0.5 3

WorldBegin
        LightSource "ambientlight" 1 "intensity" [ 0.1 ]
        LightSource "pointlight" 2
            "from" [-2 2 -2]
            "intensity" [ 7 ]

    Color [ 1 0 0 ]
    Surface "plastic"
    GeneralPolygon [4 3]
        "P"[ 0 0 0
            1 0 0
            1 1 0
            0 1 0

            0.1 0.1 0
            0.9 0.1 0
            0.5 0.9 0]
WorldEnd
```

FIGURE 13.2. A general polygon

"Curved" Polygons

When you connect polygons together to create a more complex model, there is invariably a crease where two parts meet, as seen in the top half of Figure 13.3. While this is an accurate representation of the geometry we have passed to the renderer, this crease is undesirable if we are using polygons to approximate a curved surface. The problem is that while the two surfaces are joined together without a gap, there is still a sharp change in the orientation of the surface as seen in Figure 13.4a, which results in an obvious change in the shaded color. To make things worse, our eyes are particularly tuned to pick out these kinds of edges.

FIGURE 13.3. Phong shading

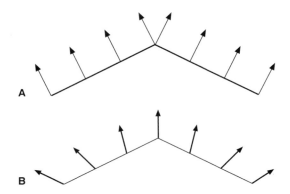

FIGURE 13.4. Surface normals

You can reduce this artifact, and create a smoother appearance by interpolating normals across the surface, as in Figure 13.4b—a technique known as Phong shading. While the surfaces are still flat, the orientation of points on the surface are faked so the points on coincident edges are not only in the same place but are shaded to have the same color. To achieve this effect in RenderMan you must explicitly assign normals to the vertices of the polygon using the "N" parameter. The polygons in the bottom half of Figure 13.3 are identical to those in the top half, but Listing 13.3 reveals that surface normals have been added so that points on the edge where the two polygons meet are shaded similarly on both sides of the join.

Listing 13.3 Phong shading.

```
#phong.rib
Display "phong.tiff" "file" "rgba"
Projection "perspective" "fov" [ 30 ]

Translate −0.5 −0.5 3

WorldBegin
    LightSource "ambientlight" 1
            "intensity" [ 0.1 ]
    LightSource "pointlight" 2
            "from" [ −2 0.5 −2 ]
            "intensity" [ 7 ]

    Color [ 1 0 0 ]
    Surface "plastic"

    #"Flat" Polygons, have a crease when joined
    Polygon "P" [ 0.0 0.55   0.0
                  0.5 0.55  −0.25
                  0.5 1.0   −0.25
                  0.0 1.0    0.0]
    Polygon "P" [ 0.5 0.55  −0.25
                  1.0 0.55   0.0
                  1.0 1.0    0.0
                  0.5 1.0   −0.25]

    #Normals Assigned to hide join'
    Polygon "P" [ 0.0 0.0   0.0
                  0.5 0.0  −0.25
                  0.5  0.45 −0.25
                  0.0  0.45  0.0]
        "N" [    0.25 0      0.5
                 0.00 0      1.0
                 0.00 0      1.0
                 0.25 0      0.5 ]
    Polygon "P" [ 0.5  0.0  −0.25
                  1.0  0.0   0.0
```

(*Continued*)

```
                            1.0   0.45   0.0
                            0.5   0.45  -0.25]
                "N"  [     0.00  0      1.0
                          -0.25  0      0.5
                          -0.25  0      0.5
                           0.00  0      1.0 ]
WorldEnd
```

The surface is shaded as if it were a smooth curve from one side to the other. However, close examination of the profile of the object reveals that it is still in fact comprised of two flat polygons. Phong shading is a useful trick that can help to hide the limitation of polygonal models but if your intention is to create a smoothly curving surface then the results will always be an approximation.

Patches

Despite their flexibility, the use of polygons is not always a good idea. Though many simple renderers handle polygons well, they do not fit comfortably into the complex shading pipeline that high quality rendering requires. You should only use polygons for objects consisting of large flat surfaces, rather than using many tiny polygons to approximate curves surfaces. RenderMan provides commands to create curved surfaces directly and wherever possible you should use these in preference.

The starting point for these curved surfaces is the humble Patch command. Before considering curved patches, however, we must look at flat patches, which are technically known as bilinear. A bilinear patch is much like a polygon but it always has four corners. While this limitation makes it more difficult to model with, there are pay-offs at the shading stage. Listing 13.4 demonstrates the creation of a patch, and generates a square identical to the polygon shown in Figure 13.1.

Listing 13.4 A patch.

```
#patch.rib
Display "patch.tiff" "file" "rgba"
Projection "perspective" "fov" [ 30 ]

Translate −0.5 −0.5 3

WorldBegin
        LightSource "ambientlight" 1 "intensity" [ 0.1]
        LightSource "pointlight" 2
            "from" [−2 2 −2]
            "intensity" [ 7 ]

    Color [ 1 0 0 ]
    Surface "plastic"
    Patch "bilinear" "P" [ 0 0 0
                          1 0 0
                          0 1 0
                          1 1 0 ]
WorldEnd
```

Though the `Patch` command may appear very similar to the Polygon command, it should be noted that a bilinear patch always has four points in the "P" array, and the order of the vertices has changed, as patches are specified a row at a time, rather than as a path around the boundary. The different ordering of points is illustrated in Figure 13.5. Unlike polygons, patches need not be planer, and hence we can create patches like the one in Listing 13.5. Here we have twisted the top two points so the patch is no longer planer as can be seen in Figure 13.6. The same set of points are not valid parameters to the `Polygon` command, and would not render reliably in different renderers.

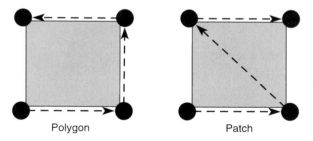

Polygon   Patch

FIGURE 13.5. Ordering of points

Listing 13.5 A curved "linear" patch.

```
#curved.rib
Display "curv ed.tiff" "file" "rgba"
Projection "perspective" "fov" [ 20 ]

Translate −0.5 −0.5 4

WorldBegin
    LightSource "ambientlight" 1 "intensity" [ 0.1 ]
    LightSource "pointlight" 2
            "from" [−2 2 −2]
            "intensity" [ 7 ]

    Color [ 1 0 0 ]
    Surface "plastic"
    Patch "bilinear" "P" [ 0    0  0
                           1    0  0
                           0.4  1  1    #MOVED BACK
                           0.6  1 −1]   #MOVED FORWARDS
WorldEnd
```

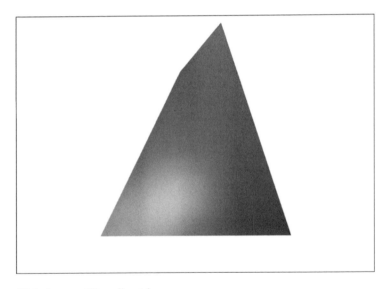

FIGURE 13.6. A curve "linear" patch

Cubic Patches

If you took nine bilinear patches and arranged them into a grid as in Figure 13.7a you could approximate a curved surface by moving those points around to form something like Figure 13.7b. However, the surface would look even better if instead of joining the points together using flat patches we could somehow fit curves through the points as in Figure 17.6c.

This is exactly what happens when we use a bicubic patch. We need 16 points, which are specified as a row at a time, as shown in Figure 13.8, to create the

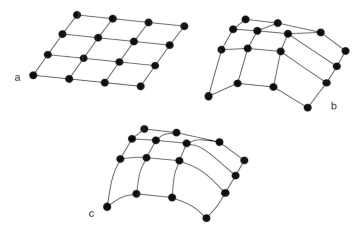

FIGURE 13.7. Joining patches: (**a**) a group of patches (**b**) approximating a curve (**c**) interpolatiging the points

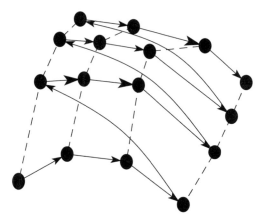

FIGURE 13.8. Control points in a cubic patch

necessary faceted surface, which is known as a control hull, and then the renderer simply fits a perfectly smooth curved surface to that hull.

We have created a bicubic patch in Listing 13.6. While it is somewhat hard to interpret, the points around the edge of the grid have been placed in a square, while the points in the centre have been displaced up and down to create an interesting surface, as seen in Figure 13.9.

Listing 13.6 A bicubic patch.

```
#cubic.rib
Display "cubic.tiff" "file" "rgba"
Projection "perspective" "fov" [ 30 ]

Translate -0.5 -0.5 3

WorldBegin
    LightSource "ambientlight" 1 "intensity" [ 0.1 ]
    LightSource "pointlight" 2
            "from" [-2 2 -2]
            "intensity" [ 10 ]

    Color [ 1 0 0 ]
    Surface "plastic"
    Rotate 40 1 0 0
    Patch "bicubic"
        "P" [ 0 0    0   0.4 0    0   0.6 0    0   1 0    0
              0 0.4  0   0.4 0.4  3   0.6 0.4 -3   1 0.4  0
              0 0.6  0   0.4 0.6 -3   0.6 0.6  3   1 0.6  0
              0 1    0   0.4 1    0   0.6 1    0   1 1    0 ]
WorldEnd
```

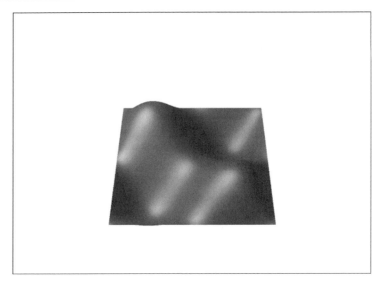

FIGURE 13.9. A bicubic patch

Rib Archives

Creating objects by hand using patches and polygons is tricky and time consuming. Of course normally models would be produced using interactive software from which a RIB file can be exported. Most software also provides an option to create RIB files containing single objects rather than a complete scene.

You can import objects into your own scene using the command `ReadArchive` followed by the name of the file, as in Listing 13.7. The contents of the archive are included in the scene at render time, just as if you had copied and pasted them into your RIB file. The imported RIB file should contain no options or other scene setup commands, but only the attribute and geometry commands to draw a specific object.

Listing 13.7 Importing an object.

```
#cubic.rib
Display "cubic.tiff" "file" "rgba"
Projection "perspective" "fov" [ 30 ]

Translate -0.5 -0.5 3

WorldBegin
    LightSource "ambientlight" 1 "intensity" [ 0.1 ]
    LightSource "pointlight" 2
            "from" [-2 2 -2]
            "intensity" [ 10 ]

    ReadArchive "teapot.rib"

WorldEnd
```

Summary

```
    Polygon ...
    GeneralPolygon [ nverts per loop ] ...
    Patch "type" ...
    ReadArchive "filename.rib"
```

Related Commands

PointsPolygons [nverts per loop] [loop verts] . . .
PointsGeneralPolygons [loops per poly] [nverts per loop] [loop verts] . . .

When polygons are used to model a surface, you inevitably have many polygons with corners and edges in common with their neighbours. Rather than passing such a surface to the renderer through a large number of separate `Polygon` commands, you can combine many polygons together in a single command using the `PointsPolygons` and `PointsGeneralPolygons` commands. By exploiting the shared vertices, the RIB file will be more compact, and the renderer can treat the set of polygons as a single object.

PatchMesh "type" nu uwrap nv vwrap . . .

In the same way you can combine polygons using `PointsPolygons`, patches are often specified in groups using the `PatchMesh` command. `PatchMesh` creates a mesh of points nu by `nv` square. This is particularly useful for bicubic patches, as it ensures that individual patches join together smoothly. By setting `uwrap` and `vwrap` to be "`periodic`" or "`nonperiodic`" you indicate if the opposite edges of the mesh should be joined together.

Basis ubasis ustep vbasis vstep

When using bicubic patches the renderer must produce a smooth curve based on the points it has been given. The exact manner in which this is done is controlled by the `Basis` command. While some methods produce curves which pass through every point, others only use the points as a guide. Some methods make it easier to stitch patches together while others give better control over the surface itself. It is possible to specify different forms of curve fitting for the rows and columns of the patch.

NuPatch nucv uorder uknot umin umax nvcvs vorder vknnot vmin vmax . . .
TrimCurve nloops ncurves order know min max n u v w

Though bicubic patch meshes are very versatile there are some forms of curvature which even they can only approximate. Yet more complex surfaces can be described using Non-Uniform Rational B-Splines (NURBS), which are generated by the `NuPatch` command. Though NURBS patches have much in common with the simpler patches, the parameters to the `NuPatch` command are probably too complex to construct by hand. Despite this complexity, the greater flexibility afforded makes NURBS surfaces the preferred primitive in most high end modeling packages. RenderMan also allows NURBS to be trimmed using the `TrimCurve` attribute—holes may be cut into the surface, and edges removed.

Chapter 14
Shadows

Introduction

The lights we have used so far have not cast any shadows. While this is acceptable for simple images, shadows are essential if any form of realism is to be established. Shadows tie objects to the surfaces they are resting on, and provide additional visual cues to the relationship of objects in a scene. In this section, we will see how shadows can be created in RenderMan.

Shadow Maps

Though most renderers now support ray traced shadows, the standard method of creating shadows in RenderMan is through the use of shadow maps. This approach is slightly tedious to setup by hand, but it does offer better performance and greater flexibility. Most modeling software can ask RenderMan to generate these maps automatically so there is little additional work for the end user.

The principle of a shadow map is to create a file that contains information about which points are in shadow with respect to a particular light source. To create this file the image is simply rendered from the position of the light, but rather than recording the color of each pixel the renderer records the distance from the camera to the front-most object, as illustrated in Figure 14.1. This is known as a Z buffer, and it defines a pseudosurface—objects behind this surface will be in shadow, while those infront will not. This process is repeated for each light in the scene (or at least all those that are required to cast shadows).

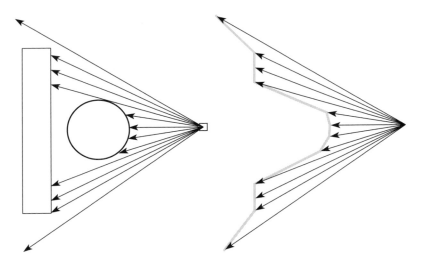

<small>FIGURE 14.1. A Z buffer</small>

Once a shadow map has been generated for the light, the main render (or beauty pass) can take place. When the renderer needs to determine if a point is in shadow with respect to a particular light, it can consult that light's shadow map. The position of the point in the shadow map is calculated, and if the point is further from the light than the distance recorded in the map it is in shadow.

Generating a Shadow Map

In practice, we might start with a simple scene consisting of an object resting on a ground plane lit by a spotlight, and an ambient fill light. Such a scene is in Listing 14.1, but as you can see in the rendered image in Figure 14.2 (also Plate V), the teapot does not cast a shadow onto the plane.

Listing 14.1 Scene without shadows.

```
#noshadow.rib
Display "noshadow.tiff" "file" "rgba"
Projection "perspective" "fov" [ 30 ]
Rotate -20 1 0 0
Translate 0 -1 5

WorldBegin
    LightSource "ambientlight" 1 "intensity" [ 0.1 ]
    LightSource "spotlight" 2
        "from" [ 0 4 0 ]
        "to" [ 0 0 0 ]
        "intensity" [ 7 ]
        "coneangle" [0.3]
        "conedeltaangle" [0.05]
    Surface "plastic"
    ReadArchive "teapot.rib"

    Color [ 0 1 0 ]
    Patch "bilinear" "P" [-5 -1 -5
                           5 -1 -5
                          -5 -1  5
                           5 -1  5]
WorldEnd
```

FIGURE 14.2. Scene without shadows (also Plate V)

To add a shadow to the spot the first thing we need to do is render a Z buffer from the position of the spotlight. This is done by placing the camera at the position of the light. When viewed from this position the scene appears as in Figure 14.3 (also Plate V).

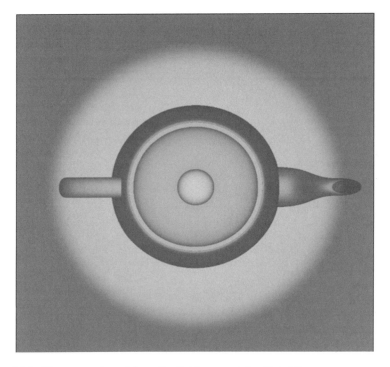

FIGURE 14.3. The scene viewed from the light source (also Plate V)

Rather than recording the color of each pixel we modify the Display command, instructing the renderer to record "z", the distances to the visible surfaces as in Listing 14.2. We have also changed the output type from `file` to `zfile`, though this is not necessary for all renderers. As the light casts a conical beam, the `Format` command has been modified to create a square image, capturing all of the points that the light illuminates. The result of this render is an image that is dark where there is a surface close to the camera and brighter where objects are further away, as shown in Figure 14.4.

Listing 14.2 Creating the Z buffer image.

```
#makeshadow.rib
Display "zbuffer.tiff" "zfile" "z"
Format 512 512 1.0
Clipping 1 10

Projection "perspective" "fov" [ 40 ]

Translate 0 0 4
Rotate -90 1 0 0

WorldBegin
    ReadArchive "teapot.rib"

    Patch "bilinear" "P" [ -5 -1 -5
                           5 -1 -5
                          -5 -1  5
                           5 -1  5 ]
WorldEnd
MakeShadow "zbuffer.tiff" "map.shad"
```

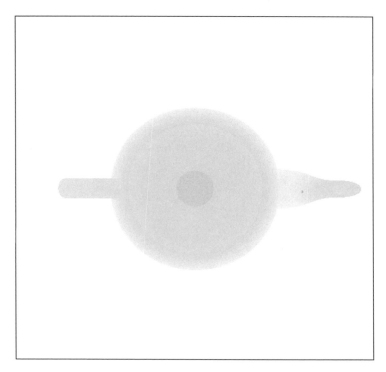

FIGURE 14.4. The Z buffer image

In addition to the depth information, a shadow map also needs to contain information about the camera it was rendered with to enable points to be correctly looked up. Camera information is combined with the depth information by the MakeShadow command, on the last line of Listing 14.2. This takes a *Z* buffer that has been rendered and adds the necessary details before writing it to a shadow map file. The field of view of the camera need not be the same as the angle of the light, and the orientation need not be the same, though significant variation would result in wasted time rendering the unused information.

You can use *Z* buffer images for many purposes besides shadows. By recording the depth of each pixel as well as its color, effects such as fogging, and depth of field can be added to a scene as a 2D postprocess. Such an approach is often preferred in a commercial production, as it allows the depth effect to be quickly changed at the compositing stage without re-rendering the scene.

Applying a Shadow Map

Having created the shadow map we now return to the original version of the scene and replace the "spotlight" with a light of type "shadowspot", as in Listing 14.3. This behaves identically to a normal spotlight except that it casts

Listing 14.3 Scene with shadows.

```
#withshadow.rib
Display "withshadow.tiff" "file" "rgba"
Projection "perspective" "fov" [ 30 ]

Rotate -20 1 0 0
Translate 0 -1 5
WorldBegin
    LightSource "ambientlight" 1 "intensity" [ 0.1 ]
    LightSource "shadowspot" 2
        "shadowname" [ "map.shad" ]
            "from" [ 0 4 0 ]
            "to" [ 0 0 0 ]
            "intensity" [ 7 ]
            "coneangle" [0.3]
            "conedeltaangle" [0.05]

    Surface "plastic"
    ReadArchive "teapot.rib"

    Color [ 0 1 0 ]
    Patch "bilinear" "P" [ -5 -1 -5
                           5 -1 -5
                          -5 -1  5
                           5 -1  5 ]

WorldEnd
```

shadows based on the map passed in by the parameter "`shadowname`." Rendering with the new light produces the image found in Figure 14.5 (also Plate V). If your renderer does not support a light of type `shadowspot` try adding the `shadowname` parameter to a regular spotlight, as some systems have chosen to replace the standard `spotlight` with one that supports shadows, rather than add a second light type.

FIGURE 14.5. Scene with shadows (also Plate V)

Note that the shadows are cast by the objects in the map, not by the geometry in the final render, so if an object is required not to cast a shadow, it should simply not be included in the RIB used to generate the map. Similarly, in Listing 14.4 we have removed the teapot from the scene, but it is still included in the shadow map. The image in Figure 14.6 (also Plate V), therefore, still contains the shadow of the removed object.

Listing 14.4 Shadow without an object.

```
#noteapot.rib
Display "noteapot.tiff" "file" "rgba"
Projection "perspective" "fov" [ 30 ]
Rotate -20 1 0 0
Translate 0 -1 5

WorldBegin
    LightSource "ambientlight" 1 "intensity" [ 0.1 ]
    LightSource "shadowspot" 2
        "shadowname" [ "map.shad" ]
```

(Continued)

```
                    "from"  [ 0  4  0 ]
                    "to"  [ 0  0  0 ]
                    "intensity"  [ 7 ]
                    "coneangle"  [0.3]
                    "conedeltaangle"  [0.05]

     Surface "plastic"
     Color [ 0  1  0 ]
     Patch "bilinear" "P" [ -5 -1 -5
                            5 -1 -5
                           -5 -1  5
                            5 -1  5 ]

WorldEnd
```

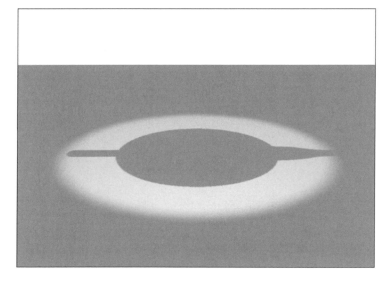

FIGURE 14.6. Shadow without an object (also Plate V)

You can also make point lights cast shadows in a similar fashion using the shadowpoint light shader, but six shadow maps are required to cover the faces of a cube enclosing the light. Multiple shadow maps may also be used to handle semitransparent objects.

Ray-Traced Shadows

While depth-mapped shadows are fast and efficient, for certain effects it is more practical to ray trace shadows—in cases where the object is semitransparent for example. Ray-traced shadows explicitly test the path between the surface and the light source to see if any objects are blocking the light. As might be expected, this can be particularly time consuming as every other object in the scene must be tested to see if it is the one blocking the light path. To enable ray-traced shadows for a particular light source you simply need to set the shadow-name parameter (which usually represents a shadow map file) to be "raytrace," as in Listing 14.5. This produces an image similar to Figure 14.5 in a single pass, but that pass may take longer than the two passes required when using shadow maps.

Listing 14.5 Ray-traced shadows.

```
#raytrace.rib
Display "raytrace.tiff" "file" "rgba"
Projection "perspective" "fov" [ 30 ]

Rotate -20 1 0 0
Translate 0 -1 5
WorldBegin
    LightSource "ambientlight" 1 "intensity" [ 0.1 ]
    LightSource "shadowspot" 2
        "shadowname" [ "raytrace" ]
        "from" [ 0 4 0 ]
        "to" [ 0 0 0 ]
        "intensity" [ 7 ]
        "coneangle" [0.3]
        "conedeltaangle" [0.05]

    Surface "plastic"
    Attribute "visibility" "transmission" [ "opaque" ]
    ReadArchive "teapot.rib"

    Color [ 0 1 0 ]
    Attribute "visibility" "transmission" [ "transparent" ]
    Patch "bilinear" "P" [ -5 -1 -5
                           5 -1 -5
                          -5 -1  5
                           5 -1  5 ]

WorldEnd
```

To speed this process up not all objects are considered as potential casters of shadows. For example, in the case of our example scene the teapot can cast shadows, but the ground plane cannot cast shadows on the teapot or itself, so in

Listing 14.5 the ground is marked with the visibility attribute that it is transparent to ray traced shadows, while the teapot is marked as opaque. This is discussed further in Chapter 30.

Summary

```
MakeShadow "zBufferFilename" "ShadowMapFilename"
LightSource "shadowspot" handle
    "from" [ x y z ]
    "to" [ x y z ]
    "intensity" [ val ]
    "color" [ r g b ]
    "coneangle" [ angle ]
    "conedeltaangle" [angle]
    "shadowname" ["Filename"]
Attribute "visibility"
    "transmission" ["transparent"]
Attribute "visibility"
    "transmission" ["opaque"]
```

Related Commands

FrameBegin framenumber
FrameEnd

The creation of shadow maps can be done in the same RIB file as the beauty pass by use of `FrameBegin` and `FrameEnd`, which allow multiple frames to be stored in the same file. Simply place `FrameBegin/End` around those commands which relate to each frame.

Display "ShadowMapFilename" "shadow" "z"

The standard method of shadow map creation is to first generate an interim Z buffer file which is then converted to a shadow map by the `MakeShadow` command. In most implementations of RenderMan, however, you can streamline this process by specifying an output device of type "shadow." When this is used, the image written to disc automatically gets the appropriate camera information added, and the `MakeShadow` command becomes obsolete.

Chapter 15
Motion Blur and Depth of Field

Introduction

Photorealism in computer generated images is often dependent not on accurately modeling the real world, but in recreating the viewers' expectations of what an image of the real world should look like. Real world images are captured using cameras which have physical limitations and defects, while the simulated digital camera can easily be made theoretically perfect. High quality photorealistic renderers must allow the user to specify a more complex camera model which reintroduces the artifacts that users expect to see in photographs and films.

In this section, we will see how the physical limitations of a real camera can be introduced back into the "perfect" virtual camera normally found in computer graphics to produce a more realistic image.

Motion Blur

Setting up the Shutter

While the simulated camera is perfectly capable of capturing the scene instantly, a real camera needs to expose light onto a film. The camera's shutter must be open for a length of time to allow enough light to enter the lens so that an image can be created. Any objects which are moving while the shutter is open will appear blurred. Any movement of the camera will result in the blurring of the whole scene.

The length of exposure is a property of the camera and hence applies to the whole scene, making it an Option that you must specify prior to `WorldBegin`. The command to specify this is `Shutter`, which takes two parameters: the time at which the shutter opens and the time at which the shutter closes. The absolute values of these parameters have no effect, but simply provide a reference for defining motion, and therefore simplicity we can set them as `Shutter 0.0 1.0`—the shutter opens at time zero and closes at time one.

Note that in a real camera the timing of the shutter would significantly affect the brightness of the image, but here the two effects have been decoupled allowing you to set each to its optimal value. The `Exposure` command controls brightness while the `Shutter` command only affects motion blur. Though in a real camera the controls interact in complex ways this only makes operation more difficult, and separating the features like this provides greater flexibility.

Defining Motion

When motion blur is in use, most of the scene will still be rendered normally, blur only being applied to those objects which are moving. Objects are positioned by the use of transformations, and hence you can specify that objects are moving by providing a pair of transforms, representing the object's position at the start and end of the shutter period. To indicate that a pair of transformations is a motion rather than simply two consecutive transforms you should enclose them within the commands `MotionBegin` and `MotionEnd`.

This is demonstrated in Listing 15.1, which contain a propeller rotating 30° about the *x*-axis in the time period 0–1. The image rendered with and without motion blur is shown in Figure 15.1. Each motion block must contain exactly

Listing 15.1 Transformation motion blur.

```
Display "motion.tiff" "file" "rgba"
Shutter 0 1

Format 640 240 1.0
Projection "perspective" "fov" 30

Rotate 90 0 1 0
Translate -5 0 0

WorldBegin
LightSource "ambientlight" 1        "intensity" [.3]
LightSource "distantlight" 2        "from" [5 10 -10]
                                    "to" [0 0 0]
                                    "intensity" [0.7]

MotionBegin [0 1]
    Rotate -15 1 0 0
    Rotate 15 1 0 0
MotionEnd
ReadArchive "prop.rib"
WorldEnd
```

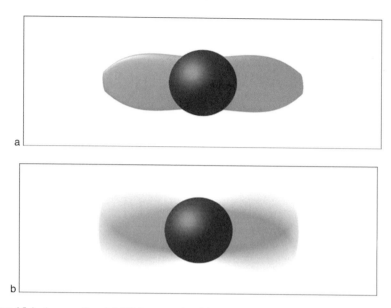

FIGURE 15.1. A propeller: (**a**) Without motion blur. (**b**) With motion blur

one set of transforms, so if an object was both spinning and translating, two consecutive motion blocks would be used, one for the `Rotate` and one for the `Translate`.

Depending on the renderer you are using it may be possible to specify more complex motion paths by positioning the object at several locations during the exposure, as shown in Listing 15.2, where a sphere is translated up and then back down, as it moves from left to right. The resulting image is in Figure 15.2. The array following `MotionBegin` contains a list of sample times, and there should be one transformation in the block for each. Separate motion blocks may contain different numbers of samples, at different times, from which the renderer will calculate the resulting motion.

Listing 15.2 A more complex motion path.

```
#path.rib
Display "path.tiff" "file" "rgba"
Projection "perspective" "fov" [ 30 ]
Shutter 0 1
Translate 0 0 3
WorldBegin
    LightSource "ambientlight" 1 "intensity" [ 0.1 ]
    LightSource "pointlight" 2
            "from" [ -2 4 -2 ]
            "intensity" [ 10 ]

    MotionBegin [ 0 0.5 1 ]
        Translate -0.5 0   0
        Translate  0.0 0.2 0
        Translate  0.5 0   0
    MotionEnd
    Color [ 1 0 0 ]
    Surface "plastic"
    Sphere 0.5 -0.5 0.5 360
WorldEnd
```

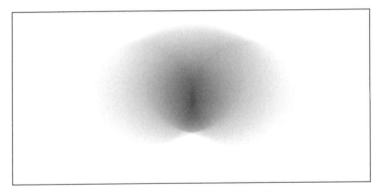

FIGURE 15.2. A more complex motion path

Deformation Blur

In addition to the blurring of objects due to transformations, objects may also require blurring because they are changing shape. You can achieve this effect in a similar way to transformation blur by placing several instances of the object inside a motion block. This is demonstrated in Listing 15.3, where a sphere decreases in size while the shutter is open.

Listing 15.3 Deformation motion blur.

```
#deform.rib
Display "deform.tiff" "file" "rgba"
Projection "perspective" "fov" [ 30 ]
Shutter 0 1

Translate 0 0 5

WorldBegin
    LightSource "ambientlight" 1 "intensity" [ 0.1 ]
    LightSource "spotlight" 2
            "from" [ -2 4 -2 ]
            "to" [ 0 0 0 ]
            "intensity" [ 10 ]
    Color [ 1 0 0 ]
    Surface "plastic"
    MotionBegin [ 0 1 ]
        Sphere 1.0 -1.0 1.0 360
        Sphere 0.5 -0.5 0.5 360
    MotionEnd
WorldEnd
```

In principle, it should be possible to motion blur the parameters to virtually any command using this approach, though the level of support for motion blur is variable between renderers. Most support the blurring of transformations, though fewer support deformation. Not all renderers support sample times other than the start and end of the shutter period, and many have problems with nonlinear paths such as those generated by motion blurring a rotation.

Depth of Field

An effect similar to motion blur is depth of field. Again, it is an artifact of real cameras that we must mimic in our computer-generated imagery so it meets the cinematic expectations of the audience. Only objects that are at a certain distance from the camera are in focus, and any object significantly closer or further away will appear blurred. Though complex to calculate, depth of field provides important visual cues about the relationship of objects and may also be used for dramatic effect.

Depth of field is specified by the option command `DepthOfField` which takes three parameters: the f-stop, the focal length, and the focal distance. While these parameters are very familiar to traditional photographers, and allow the camera to be matched to live action shots for effects work, they are somewhat confusing when first encountered in a pure computer graphics context.

Focal Distance

The simplest parameter is `focaldistance`. This is simply the distance from the camera at which objects will be perfectly in focus. By animating this parameter over several frames you can draw the attention of the audience from one object to another.

In order to relate synthetic depth of field to the real world effect, we will assume that one unit in the RIB file corresponds to 1m. Listing 15.4 sets up a row of spheres at distances from 1 to 7m. It also includes a depth of field command. The third parameter of `DepthOfField` specifies the focal distance and this has initially been set to 2. The resulting image in Figure 15.3a shows that the third sphere from the front is in sharp focus while those further back are increasingly blurred. By contrast in Figure 15.3b we have moved the focal distance back to 5m, using the command `DepthOfField 2.8 0.100 5` resulting in a highly blurred foreground.

Listing 15.4 Depth of field.

```
#near.rib
Display "near.tiff" "file" "rgba"
Projection "perspective" "fov" [ 30 ]

DepthOfField 2.8 0.100 2

Translate 0 0 1

WorldBegin
#1 Meter
     Translate 0.3 0 0
     Color [ 1 0 0 ]
     Sphere 0.25 -0.25 0.25 360

     Translate -0.2 0 0.5
     Color [ 0 1 0 ]
     Sphere 0.25 -0.25 0.25 360

     Translate -0.2 0 0.5
     Color [ 0 0 1 ]
     Sphere 0.25 -0.25 0.25 360

     Translate -0.2 0 0.5
     Color [ 1 0 0 ]
     Sphere 0.25 -0.25 0.25 360

#3 Meters
     Translate -0.2 0 0.5
     Color [ 0 1 0 ]
     Sphere 0.25 -0.25 0.25 360

     Translate -0.2 0 0.5
     Color [ 0 0 1 ]
     Sphere 0.25 -0.25 0.25 360
```

```
        Translate -0.2 0 0.5
        Color [ 1 0 0 ]
        Sphere 0.25 -0.25 0.25 360

        Translate -0.2 0 0.5
        Color [ 0 1 0 ]
        Sphere 0.25 -0.25 0.25 360
#5 Meters
        Translate -0.2 0 0.5
        Color [ 0 0 1 ]
        Sphere 0.25 -0.25 0.25 360

        Translate -0.2 0 0.5
        Color [ 1 0 0 ]
        Sphere 0.25 -0.25 0.25 360

        Translate -0.2 0 0.5
        Color [ 0 1 0 ]
        Sphere 0.25 -0.25 0.25 360

        Translate -0.2 0 0.5
        Color [ 0 0 1 ]
        Sphere 0.25 -0.25 0.25 360
WorldEnd
```

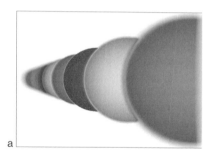 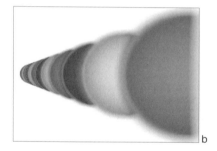

a   b

FIGURE 15.3. (a) A short focal distance of 2m (b) A larger focal distance of 5m (also Plate VI)

Focal length

The `focallength` parameter is a property of a particular lens, as it describes the extent to which it bends light. When using a real 35mm camera, a typical wide-angle lens might have a focal length of 35mm while a telephoto lens could be 200mm or greater. All things being equal, a longer lens will produce a more blurred image, as only those objects very close to the focal distance are in focus. A shorter lens is more forgiving, and objects stay sharp over a larger range of distances.

In order to demonstrate this we have used a focal distance of 4m so the spheres in the centre of the row will be in focus. In Figure 15.4a we have used a 60mm lens (`DepthOfField 2.8 0.060 4`) corresponding to a typical medium lens while the image in Figure 15.4b uses a 150 mm lens lens (`DepthOfField 2.8 0.150 4`). As you can see in Figure 15.4a, all the spheres except the closest are in sharp focus, while in Figure 15.4b the foreground is extremely out of focus, and some blurring can be seen in the last two spheres.

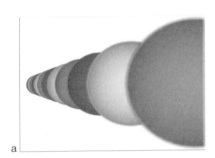 

a   b

FIGURE 15.4. (**a**) A short focal length. (**b**) A long focal length (also Plate VI)

F-Stop

Perhaps the most confusing parameter for the nonphotographer is the `f-stop`. However, put most simply: a small `f-stop` value will produce a lot of blurring, while a larger `f-stop` value will produce less. In a real camera, suitable values might be between 1.8 and 22, but this need only be a starting point for experimentation. In the images used so far, a `f-stop` of 2.8 has been used to ensure that the effect is noticeable, but in practice a larger value would often be used. Figure 15.5a uses a 100 mm lens, focused at 4m with an `f-stop` of 2.8, lens (`DepthOfField 2.8 0.100 4`) and produces obvious blurring in the image. However, in the otherwise identical Figure 15.5b we have increased the `f-stop` to 8 (`DepthOfField 8 0.100 4`) and the image is significantly sharper. Taken to the extreme, a very large `f-stop` will remove depth of field effects completely.

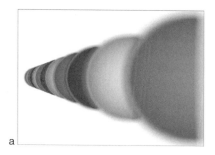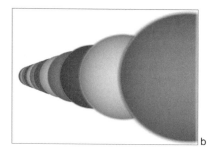

a
b

FIGURE 15.5. (**a**) A small f-stop value (**b**) A large f-stop value (also Plate VI)

In a real camera f-stop is related to the size of the aperture, and hence how much light can enter the camera. Specifying the focal length of the lens also implicitly controls the field of view. However, as was the case for motion blur, these effects are decoupled in the synthetic camera, allowing you to control image brightness and field of view with Exposure and Projection, respectively.

Summary

```
Shutter starttime endtime
MotionBegin [ sampletimes... ]
MotionEnd
DepthOfField f-stop focallength focaldistance
```

Chapter 16
The C API

Introduction

Having established the basic concepts of describing scenes to a renderer using the RIB file format, we can now transfer that knowledge to the more complex, but more powerful C form of the RenderMan interface.

Overview

The RIB file format is an effective way to distribute scenes for rendering, but as a method of generating geometry it can be a little tedious. To create 100 spheres you would need to type the `Sphere` command 100 times into the RIB file. Specifying large numbers of coordinates for patches and polygons by hand is also highly error prone. While viewing and modifying RIB files is a powerful technique of debugging and adapting renders, most RIBs are generated automatically by programs. Even if you are not planning to write your own programs, much of the documentation of RenderMan is written in terms of the C API, and so understanding the nature of the C interface is invaluable.

The C API consists of a set of functions declared in the header file "`ri.h`", which are called by the user's code. Each of these functions corresponds to a single RIB command, and hence adapting between the two interfaces is relatively straightforward. When the program is compiled it is linked with a RIB library so that when the program is run, a RIB file is written to disk which can then be rendered in the usual way. This process is shown graphically in Figure 16.1. It may also be possible to link directly to your renderer, in which case running the program will generate the image in a single step.

Of course it is also perfectly practical to generate RIBs by simply printing out the relevant commands. Though this may appear a little simpler at first, using the official functions provides an additional level of error checking, and flexibility.

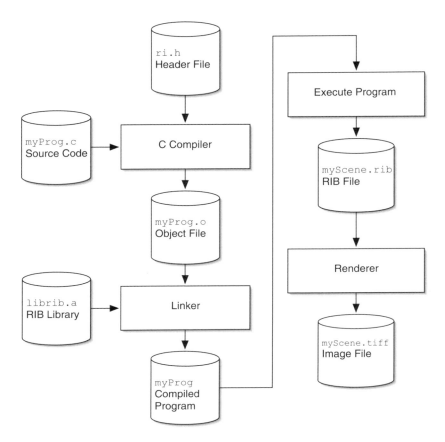

FIGURE 16.1. Compiling a RenderMan C program

A first C Program

A RenderMan client program must call the function RiBegin() before any other RenderMan function in order to initialize the renderer, and it must end by calling RiEnd(). Between these function calls you can execute the rendering commands you have used in RIB files, by calling functions whose names are the same as in RIBs but with the prefix Ri (Rendering Interface) attached. For example a sphere is created by the function RiSphere(). A C program that will generate our first RIB file (Listing 6.1) is shown in Listing 16.1.

Listing 16.1 A simple C program.

```
/* min.c - a minimal C program to use RenderMan */
#include <ri.h>

int main(int argc, char *argv[])
{

RiBegin(RI_NULL);
    RiDisplay ("min.tiff", "file", "rgba",RI_NULL);
    RiProjection ("perspective",RI_NULL);
    RiWorldBegin();
        RiTranslate(0,0,2);
        RiSphere(1,-1,1,360,RI_NULL);
    RiWorldEnd();
RiEnd();
return 0;
}
```

As there is a direct correspondence between RIB commands and C functions, all of the previous techniques described in RIB form can be applied in C. The C API is more flexible, however, as we can use C code to generate RIBs that are far more complex than you could ever hope to produce by hand. For example, to generate a RIB similar to Listing 15.4, which we used to explore depth of field, you would use a for loop as in Listing 16.2. To extend the line of spheres indefinitely is trivial in the C code, but incredibly tedious using RIB.

Listing 16.2 Using a for loop

```
/* loop.c - Create a line of Spheres */
#include <ri.h>

int main(int argc, char *argv[])
{
int i;
RiBegin(RI_NULL);
    RiDisplay ("loop.tiff", "file", "rgba",RI_NULL);
    RiProjection ("perspective",RI_NULL);
    RiDepthOfField(2.8,0.100,2);
    RiTranslate(0,0,1);
    RiWorldBegin();
        RiTranslate(0.3,0,0);
        for(i=0;i<12;i++)
            {
            RiSphere(0.25,-0.25,0.25,360,RI_NULL);
            RiTranslate(-0.2,0,0.5);
            }
    RiWorldEnd();
RiEnd();
return 0;
}
```

Parameter Lists

The C language has a far more complex syntax than the RIB file format which is simply a list of explicit commands. Because of the increased flexibility, the C API cannot always guess what we are trying to do in the same way as the renderer can, and hence it occasionally needs extra hints. In particular, parameter lists such as the parameters of a shader are somewhat tricky to handle. As in RIB files, a C parameter list consists of tokens (parameter names) and values (arrays of data). In C, however, values are always passed to the renderer through pointers, which can produce somewhat convoluted code. Typically an array is created which contains the values, and then the array is passed to the Ri function.

The C language also needs some method of knowing how many different parameters are in each list. This is done by terminating the list with RI_NULL. You must make sure you include this at the end of each parameter list, as failure to do so will cause your program to crash. Listing 16.3 demonstrates a simple

Listing 16.3 Passing a parameter list.

```
/* param.c - create a linear */
#include <ri.h>

int main(int argc, char *argv[])
{
RtPoint square[4]={{0,0,0},{1,0,0},{0,1,0},{1,1,0}};
RtColor red={1,0,0};
float fov=30;

RiBegin(RI_NULL);
    RiDisplay ("param.tiff", "file", "rgba",RI_NULL);
    RiProjection("perspective",
                     "fov",&fov,
                     RI_NULL);
    RiTranslate(-0.5,-0.5,3);
    RiWorldBegin();
        RiColor(red);
        RiPatch("bilinear",
                     "P",square,
                     RI_NULL);
    RiWorldEnd();
RiEnd();
return 0;
}
```

parameter list which we've used to create a linear patch similar to that in Listing 13.4. Listing 16.3 also uses a parameter to specify the field of view. You should note that even though "fov" only takes a single float value it is still passed via a pointer. Colors are passed using the type RtColor, which is, again, actually an array.

Many commands that we have already used support parameter lists even though we have safely ignored them when using the RIB API. For example, all geometry commands can use parameter lists to specify "varying" parameters. While most properties of an object are "uniform" in that they apply to the whole surface, we sometimes want an attribute to change over the surface. In Listing 16.4 we use a varying value of "Cs" (the shading language name for the surface color) on a Patch. Each of the four colors is attached to a corner of the patch and blended across it, replacing the uniform color specified by the Color command in Figure 16.2 (also Plate VI). You can use the same approach to vary other shader parameters over a surface, but they must be declared as "varying" in the shader.

Listing 16.4 Blending colors on a surface.

```
#cubic.rib
Display "cubic.tiff" "file" "rgb"
Projection "perspective" "fov" [ 30 ]
Translate 0 0 3
WorldBegin
LightSource "ambientlight" 1
     "intensity" [ 0.1]
LightSource "pointlight" 2
        "from"    [ 2 2 2]
        "intensity" [ 10 ]
Surface "plastic"
Rotate 40 1 0 0
Translate -0.5 -0.5 0
Patch "bicubic" "P" [0 0    0  0.4 0    0  0.6 0    0  1 0    0
                     0 0.4 0  0.4 0.4 -3  0.6 0.4  3  1 0.4 0
                     0 0.6 0  0.4 0.6  3  0.6 0.6 -3  1 0.6 0
                     0 1    0  0.4 1    0  0.6 1    0  1 1    0]
          "Cs" [    1 0 0
                    0 1 0
                    0 0 1
                    1 1 1 ]
WorldEnd
```

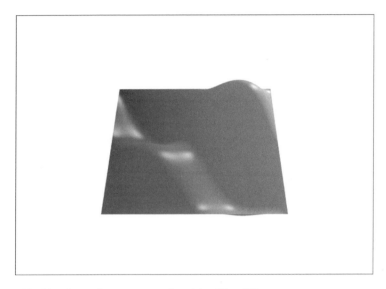

FIGURE 16.2. Blending colors over a surface (also Plate VI)

Declaring Parameter Types

In the case of the patch used in Listing 16.3, it is relatively clear that the array "P" must contain four elements, each being a point. In many cases, however, there may be no way of interpreting a parameter without additional information. For example, a shader which takes a parameter "x", might define "x" as either a color, a float, or even an array of floats. The only way to determine this would be by reference to the shader itself.

While most renderers are capable of extracting this information, you usually need to provide the C API with a hint to tell it how to handle each value passed into it. The function RiDeclare can be used to specify the type of a variable before it is passed through the C API. This is demonstrated in Listing 16.5 where the surface shader "myConstantSurface," requires a parameter "customColor" of type "uniform color." You can usually find the correct type of a variable by reference to the documentation or shader source.

Listing 16.5 Declaring a parameter type.

```
/*declare.c - declare the type of a shader parameter*/
#include <ri.h>

int main(int argc, char *argv[])
{
RtPoint square[4]={{0,0,0},{1,0,0},{0,1,0},{1,1,0}};
RtColor red={1,0,0};
float fov=30;
```

```
RiBegin(RI_NULL);
    RiDisplay ("declare.tiff","file", "rgba",RI_NULL);
    RiProjection ("perspective",
                    "fov",&fov,
                    RI_NULL);
    RiTranslate(-0.5,-0.5,3);
    RiWorldBegin();
        RiDeclare("customColor","uniform color");
        RiSurface("myConstantSurface",
                    "customColor",red,
                    RI_NULL);
        RiPatch("bilinear",
                    "P",square,
                    RI_NULL);
    RiWorldEnd();
RiEnd();
return 0;
}
```

As an alternative to `RiDeclare` you can include the parameter type in the paramteter name:

```
    RiSurface("myConstantSurface",
        "uniform color customColor",red,
        RI_NULL).
```

Both this format and `Declare` can also be used in RIB files, though depending on your renderer you may not be required to use them as often as when programming C.

Certain other functions explicitly require hints as additional parameters. For example, the RIB command `Polygon` can work out for itself the number of points in the polygon, but the C equivalent `RiPolygon` function requires the number of vertices as its first parameter.

Light Sources

When you declare light sources in a RIB file you must specify a handle, so that you can refer to the same light later in the file. The C API uses the same concept but rather than the user providing their own handle, the handle is calculated by the `RiLightSource()` function and passed back to the user as a variable of type `RtLightHandle`. To create a light you therefore need to use code like that in Listing 16.6.

Listing 16.6 Declaring a light.

```
/* light.c - create a light source */
#include <ri.h>

int main(int argc, char *argv[])
{
RtPoint square[4]={{0,0,0},{1,0,0},{0,1,0},{1,1,0}};
RtPoint lightPos[1]={{0,0,-0.2}};
RtLightHandle theLight;
RtColor red={1,0,0};
float fov=30;

RiBegin(RI_NULL);
    RiDisplay ("light.tiff","file","rgb",RI_NULL);
    RiProjection ("perspective",
              "fov",&fov,
              RI_NULL);
    RiTranslate(-0.5,-0.5,3);
    RiWorldBegin();
        theLight = RiLightSource("pointlight",
                    "from",lightPos,
                    RI_NULL);
        RiColor(red);
        RiPatch("bilinear",
             "P",square,
             RI_NULL);
    RiWorldEnd();
RiEnd();
return 0;
}
```

Summary

```
RiBegin(RI_NULL);
RiEnd();
RiSphere(rad,zmin,zmax,theta,...,RI_NULL);
RiPatch("type",...,RI_NULL);
RiPolygon(nverts,...,RI_NULL);
RiColor(color);
RiDeclare("varName","varType");
RtLightHandle myLight=RiLightSource("type",...,
    RI_NULL);
```

Chapter 17
Particles and Hair

Introduction

When modeling dust, explosions, fur, hair, and other similar phenomena we often require not hundreds of surfaces but perhaps tens or hundreds of thousands. In order to deal with these demands Points and Curves primitives were added to the RenderMan standard. In this chapter, we will look at how you can use these to describe objects which are too fine to require a full 3D model, in a highly efficient manner.

Particles

Particles are one of the most commonly used tools in the special effects industry, creating smoke, fire, dust, rain, and countless other phenomena. These illusions rely not on the appearance of the individual particles but rather the combined image of thousands of particles or more. While it is possible to render each of these particles as a simple object such as a sphere, the `Points` command is designed to render a complete particle system as a single piece of geometry, and in doing so greatly improves efficiency.

Because particles are designed to be used in huge numbers it makes little sense to create them by hand in a RIB file. Using the C API it is trivial to create any number of points. In Listing 17.1, we fill the array "`position`" with 1,000 coordinates generated by sine and cosine waves of different frequencies. In the second half of the code we simply pass this to the `Points` command using the "`P`" parameter. As we are using the C API we also need to specify how many points there are, though in a RIB file this is not necessary. When the program is run a RIB file is generated, which can be rendered to produce Figure 17.1.

Listing 17.1 The Points command.

```c
/* point.c - create a simple Particle System */
#include <ri.h>
#include <math.h>

#define COUNT 1000
#define JITTER(SCALE) (((random()%1000)/500.0-1)*SCALE)

int main(int argc, char *argv[])
{
RtPoint position[COUNT];
RtColor red={1,0,0};
float fov=30;
int i;

/*Generate Particle Postions*/
for(i=0;i<COUNT;i++)
    {
    position[i][0]=sin(i*0.5)*50+JITTER(2);
    position[i][1]=cos(i*0.1)*50+JITTER(2);
    position[i][2]=cos(i*0.5)*100+JITTER(2);
    }

RiBegin(RI_NULL);
    RiDisplay ("point.tiff","file","rgba",RI_NULL);
    RiProjection ("perspective",
            "fov",&fov,
            RI_NULL);
    RiWorldBegin();
        RiTranslate(0,0,300);
        RiColor(red);
        RiPoints(COUNT, "P", position, RI_NULL);
    RiWorldEnd();
RiEnd();
return 0;
}
```

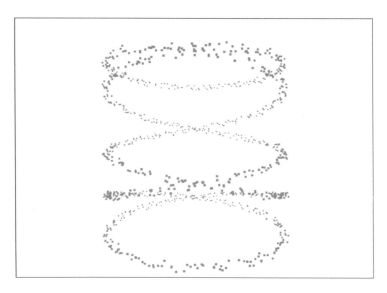

FIGURE 17.1. The points command

Particle Size

By default, particles have a width of 1, and hence in Listing 17.1 we had to translate the particles system back from the camera by 300 units to ensure that the particles were sufficiently small. In Listing 17.2, however, we have taken control over the size of the particles. We have created two sets of points here, and in the first—which is colored red—we have set the size of particles using the parameter "constantwidth." This sets a uniform size for every point in the group. Should you need to set the size of each particle individually you can do this, as we have in the case of the second (green) set of points, using the "varying" parameter "width," which allows us to specifiy a size for each particle. The resulting image is shown in Figure 17.2.

Listing 17.2 Controlling the size of points.

```
/* width.c - Create Particles of different sizes*/
#include <ri.h>
#include <math.h>
#define COUNT 2000
#define JITTER(SCALE) (((random()%1000)/500.0-1)*SCALE)

int main(int argc, char *argv[])
{
RtPoint position[COUNT];
RtColor red={1,0,0};
RtColor green={0,1,0};
float width[COUNT];
float constantwidth=0.5;
float fov=30;
int i;
/*Generate Particle Postions*/
for(i=0;i<COUNT;i++)
    {
    position[i][0]=sin(i*0.5)*50+JITTER(2);
    position[i][1]=cos(i*0.1)*50+JITTER(2);
    position[i][2]=cos(i*0.5)*100+JITTER(2);
    width[i]=JITTER(0.5)+0.5;
    }
RiBegin(RI_NULL);
    RiDisplay ("width.tiff","file","rgba",RI_NULL);
    RiProjection ("perspective",
            "fov",&fov,
            RI_NULL);
    RiWorldBegin();
        RiTranslate(0,0,300);
        RiColor(red);
        RiPoints(COUNT/2,"P",position,
                "constantwidth", &constantwidth,
                RI_NULL);
        RiColor(green);
        RiPoints(COUNT/2,"P",position+COUNT/2,
                "width",width+COUNT/2,
                RI_NULL);
    RiWorldEnd();
RiEnd();
return 0;
}
```

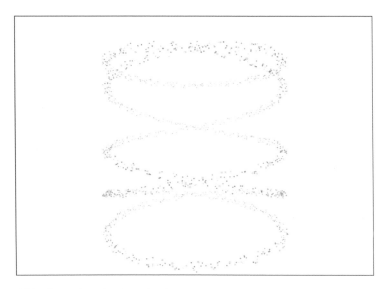

FIGURE 17.2. Controling the size of points

The varying parameter "Cs" is also invaluable when used with the Points command as it allows us to control the color of each point individually, rather than applying a single color to every particle. We've done this in Listing 17.3 which stores a random color for each point in the array "color", and passes it to the Points command as part of its parameter list. The result is shown in Figure 17.3 (also Plate VI).

Listing 17.3 Changing the color of points.

```
/* color.c - Create Particles of different colors*/
#include <ri.h>
#include <math.h>

#define COUNT 2000
#define JITTER(SCALE)  (((random()%1000)/500.0-1)*SCALE)

int main(int argc, char *argv[])
{
RtPoint position[COUNT];
RtColor color[COUNT];
float constantwidth=0.5;
float fov=30;
int i;
/*Generate Particle Postions*/
```

(*Continued*)

```
for(i=0;i<COUNT;i++)
    {
    position[i][0]=sin(i*0.5)*50+JITTER(2);
    position[i][1]=cos(i*0.1)*50+JITTER(2);
    position[i][2]=cos(i*0.5)*100+JITTER(2);
    color[i][0]=JITTER(0.5)+0.5;
    color[i][1]=JITTER(0.5)+0.5;
    color[i][2]=JITTER(0.5)+0.5;
    }
RiBegin(RI_NULL);
    RiDisplay ("color.tiff","file","rgb",RI_NULL);
    RiProjection ("perspective",
            "fov",&fov,
            RI_NULL);
    RiWorldBegin();
        RiTranslate(0,0,300);
        RiPoints(COUNT,"P",position,
                "constantwidth", &constantwidth,
                "Cs",color,
                RI_NULL);
    RiWorldEnd();
RiEnd();
return 0;
}
```

FIGURE 17.3. Changing the color of points (also Plate VI)

If you look closely you might notice that points are not rendered as true 3D objects but as small, flat flakes, which are oriented towards the camera. This is one of the optimizations which allows thousands of particles to be rendered in only a few seconds. Although the individual points are rather limited in their appearance, the intention is that points should be visible only as a cloud, not as individuals. Even though points are actually flat you can still scale, rotate and translate them as if they were real 3D objects – their flatness is an optimization which should go unnoticed. However, you must avoid making them too large on screen or else this subterfuge will be uncovered.

Hair

Rendering hair or fur has much in common with particle techniques. Once again the visual interest comes not from the complexity of the individual objects but from the large number of objects that compose an image. The Curves command takes the idea of a flat object oriented to the camera, as used for particles and extends it to render a set of curves. A curve has a length, but it has no depth, and minimal width.

We have created a set of curves in Listing 17.4. As was the case for points, we first calculate the positions of the point on each curve and store them into an array. If you wanted to create a realistic hair simulation then the complexity would lie here, in calculating the movement of the hairs, rather than in the rendering itself. The curves we have created are quite simple, and each contain four points. However, as it is possible to have a different numbers of points for each curve in a set, we also create an array nverts that we will use to tell the renderer how many points belong to each curve.

Listing 17.4 The Curves command.

```
/* curves.c - create a set of curves */
#include <ri.h>
#include <math.h>

#define COUNT 1000
#define JITTER(SCALE) (((random()%1000)/500.0-1)*SCALE)

int main(int argc, char *argv[])
{
RtPoint position[COUNT*4];
RtInt nverts[COUNT];
RtColor red={1,0,0};
float curveWidth=0.3;
float fov=30;
int i;
```

(Continued)

```
/*Generate Curve Postions*/
for(i=0;i<COUNT;i++)
    {
    float tx=(sin(i*0.3)*i*50)/COUNT+JITTER(5);
    float ty=(cos(i*0.3)*i*50)/COUNT+JITTER(5);

    position[i*4+0][0]=0;
    position[i*4+0][1]=0;
    position[i*4+0][2]=50;

    position[i*4+1][0]=0.1*tx;
    position[i*4+1][1]=0.1*ty;
    position[i*4+1][2]=25;

    position[i*4+2][0]=0.4*tx;
    position[i*4+2][1]=0.4*ty;
    position[i*4+2][2]=0;

    position[i*4+3][0]=tx;
    position[i*4+3][1]=ty;
    position[i*4+3][2]=-25;

    nverts[i]=4;
    }
RiBegin(RI_NULL);
    RiDisplay ("curves.tiff","file","rgba",RI_NULL);
    RiProjection ("perspective",
             "fov",&fov,
             RI_NULL);
    RiWorldBegin();
        RiTranslate(0,0,200);
        RiColor(red);
        RiRotate(45,1,0,0);
        RiCurves("linear",COUNT,
                nverts,
                "nonperiodic",
                "P",position,
                "constantwidth",&curveWidth,
                RI_NULL);
    RiWorldEnd();
RiEnd();
return 0;
}
```

Like patches, we can choose to either connect these points with straight lines
or fit a curve through them. The first parameter to the Curves command is therefore either "linear" or "cubic." Figure 17.4 shows the result of rendering this
set of curves with both linear and cubic interpolation. We also tell the renderer the
number of curves, and number of points in each curve, as previously calculated.
It is possible to connect the end of a curve back to its start making a small loop,
but here we have specified that the curves should be nonperiodic. Finally, we pass
in the array of points which define the curves. Like points, we can specify the
width of the curve using the parameters "constantwidth" or "width."

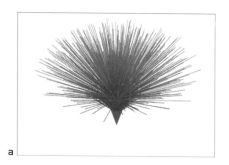
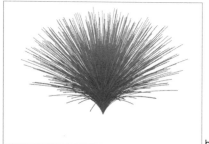

a   b

FIGURE 17.4. A set of curves: (**a**) linear (**b**) cubic

Summary

RIB API

```
Points ...
Curves "linear" [nvertices ] "nonperiodic" ...
```

C API

```
RiPoints(nPoints, ..., RI_NULL);
RiCurves("linear", ncurves, nvertices [],
     "nonperiodic",
        ..., RI_NULL);
```

Part 3
Shading

Though RenderMan supports a wide range of modeling primitives, it would be impossible to use geometry to create the level of detail required by even the simplest of scenes. Instead, fine surface detail is added to coarser base surfaces through the use of shaders. You can use RenderMan shaders to influence many stages of the rendering process, but the most common form is the surface shader. The job of the surface shader is to decide the color of each point on a surface, based upon its position, orientation, lighting and the observer. The renderer provides the shader with the necessary information to perform this calculation, and then integrates the result into the final image.

In order to maximize flexibility, shaders take the form of short fragments of computer code. While obviously being able to program helps here, a small amount of knowledge goes a long way, as most of the hard work is already being done by the renderer. Useful shaders can be very short, and algorithmically simple, as even basic shaders can produce visually interesting surfaces.

Chapter 18
My First Shader

Introduction

In this chapter we will compile and view a simple shader. In doing so, you will become familiar with the shader writing tools and processes, which we will apply to more complex examples in later chapters.

Writing the Code

RenderMan shaders are written using a special programming language know as SL (Shading Language). The code descrbing a shader called `mySurface` will typically be found in the file "`mySurface.sl`." While this naming convention is not strictly necessary, it is a very sensible convention to adopt, and we will assume it here.

The code for our first shader is in Listing 18.1. In SL anything between `/*` and `*/` is a comment, so the first line of code is simply a description of the files contents. The second line indicates that this is a shader of type "`surface`" and has the name "`first`." This is the name that it will be referred to by, in a RIB file or animation package. The rest of the file will be considered in greater detail in the following chapter.

Listing 18.1 A first shader.

```
/* A Simple Shader Shader written in SL */
surface first()
    {
    Oi=Os;
    Ci=Cs * Oi;
    }
```

The shader source code is simply text, and can be entered using any text editor, such as textedit (MacOSX), kate (Linux), or notepad (Windows). It should be saved in a text file with the name "first.sl". The exact layout is not important, so you can add new lines, or spaces wherever you choose, but it is important to lay the code out so that it is as clear and readable as possible.

Preparing the Shader for Use

In order to use the shader with a particular renderer it first needs to be transformed from the text format of the shading language into a more basic format that can be understood by the renderer—a processed known known as "compilation." This is done by a program (known as a compiler) which is unique to each RenderMan renderer. You should refer to the documentation of your renderer for the information on its compiler, but the most common examples are:

Renderer	Compiler Name	File Extension
PRMan	shader	.slo
RenderDotC	shaderdc	.system dependant
Air	shaded	.slb
3Delight	shaderdl	.sdl
Aqsis	aqsl	.slx
Angel	giles	.slc

We will use the command "shader" (the PRMan shader compiler), but you should substitute for whatever is required by your renderer. When this program is run a new file is created which contains a version of the shader optimised for a particular renderer. You would therefore compile your new surface "first" for use by PRMan using the command "shader first.sl" to create the file "first.slo." Each renderer uses a unique file extension for its compiled shaders, so you can compile a shader for several renderers and keep the results in the same folder.

If a compiled shader is not generated, this usually means there is a mistake somewhere in your shader. This will happen, even when you are proficient at shader writing, as the compiler insists that the shader be exactly right before it can be used to create an image. In the event of an error the compiler will usually print a list of problems, along with the line number of the code which caused problems.

Tackle the errors one at a time, starting with the first, as a problem on one line will often confuse the compiler, making it think there are far more problems than there are—fixing the first error will often solve all of them. If you cannot see a problem on the line that the compiler is reporting an error on, check the line before, as sometimes the compiler does not notice a mistake until slightly later than it should.

Viewing the Results

At this stage it would be possible to go into the modeling package of your choice, and use the shader. During the process of writing a shader, however, you will probably need to do this hundreds of times. It, therefore, makes sense to streamline the process as much as possible (and also avoid tying up a potentially valuable modeling licence). A good method of doing this is to either manually or using your modeling software create a RIB file which has the new shader attached to a simple object (a sphere or a plane), as in Listing 18.2. This can be rendered quickly and easily from the command line to produce something like Figure 18.1.

Listing 18.2 A test scene

```
Display "first.tiff" "file" "rgba"
Projection "perspective" "fov" [45]
LightSource "ambientlight" 1
     "intensity" [0.2]
LightSource "spotlight" 2
     "from" [-1 1 0 ]
     "to" [0 0 3]
     "intensity" [3]
Translate 0 0 3
WorldBegin
     Color [1 0 0]
     Surface "first"
     Sphere 1 -1 1 360
WorldEnd
```

FIGURE 18.1. A first shader

Starting with simple geometry allows you to understand the behavior of your shader better than a complex model would. The development process therefore becomes:

```
edit myShader.sl
shader myShader.sl
render testMyShader.rib
viewer testMyShader.tiff
rinse and repeat . . .
```

A typical shader development process might use a simple RIB file for the initial development. Once the basic look has been established a more complex RIB file can be used, perhaps containing the object for which the shader is being developed, so the appearance can be evaluated in situ. Only for final tweaking and production testing need the shader actually be loaded into the modeling package.

Summary

The shader development process is summarized in Figure 18.2.

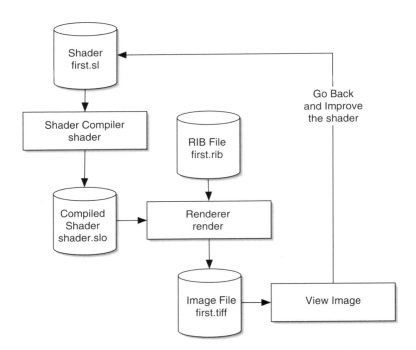

FIGURE 18.2. Compiling shaders

Chapter 19
Lighting Models

Introduction

Having successfully written and rendered a simple shader, we are now ready to start expanding the body of the code, to produce more interesting results. In this chapter, we will investigate the way that the surface interacts with the lights in the scene. You will see that some simple approximations will allow us to produce a wide range of effects that you can use as a starting point for your own shaders.

Constant

The shader "`first`," from the previous chapter, is in fact identical to one of the standard RenderMan shaders, known as "`constant`." This ignores any lights in the scene, and simply applies a flat color to the object—the color that you specified in the RIB file. The opacity of the object as defined in the RIB file is also included.

If we examine the code for "`constant`" more closely (Listing 19.1), it uses four variables Oi, Os, Cs, and Ci. O stands for opacity and C for color. Os and Cs are the values assigned by the `Color` and `Opacity` commands in the RIB file. These are passed to the surface shader by the renderer. It is the surface shader's job to take these values and calculate the color and opacity of the object

Listing 19.1 The constant shader.

```
surface constant ()
{
    Oi=Os;
    Ci=Oi * Cs;
}
```

when it is observed by the camera in particular scene. The values calculated are assigned to the variables Oi and Ci, which are then used to construct the final image. These standard variables are known as "globals," and are the standard mechanism by which data flows into and out of the shader (a summary of the global variables is on the inside back cover).

The constant shader simply takes the provided opacity (Os) and assigns it to the output opacity (Oi). The second line where the output color (Ci) is calculated is slightly more complex, as the output color is the input color multiplied by the opacity. This is known as "premultiplied" or "associated" opacity. Normally, color values range between 0 and 1, so 1,0,0 would be bright red. However, if this color was applied to a surface that was totally transparent, then the surface could not carry any color at all (0,0,0). If the surface was 50% transparent, then half the output color would come from the surface (0.5,0,0) and half would be from whatever was behind the surface. Multiplying the surface color by the opacity takes this into account. The simple rule is that you should always multiply the output color by the opacity.

Matte

In order to make a surface appear three-dimensional we need a surface shader that will take into account the position of lights and the orientation of the surface to these lights.

Surface Orientation

The orientation of a surface at a point is defined by the surface normal, which is stored in the global variable N. This variable contains a vector which points away from the surface, and has a different value at every point on the surface. We are also going to need to consider the direction from which the surface is being viewed, and this is in the variable I. Both N and I are illustrated in Figure 19.1.

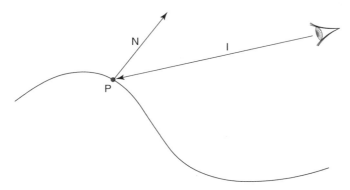

FIGURE 19.1. N and I

The variable N also tells us which side of the surface is the front and which is the back, but we probably do not care—we usually want to shade both sides of a surface in the same way. We therefore need to calculate the "face forward surface normal." If we are looking at the back of the surface, then N will be pointing away from us (in the same direction as I), so we must reverse the direction of N, and store it in a new variable "Nf". If N is already pointing towards us we can just copy it to Nf. In either case Nf will always point towards us. All of this can simply be achieved using the function faceforwards()—some code built into the renderer which performs the calulation we require, and returns the correct value of Nf:

```
normal Nf=faceforwards(N,I);
```

Nf is declared as a variable of type "normal," since although it is a vector we are going to use it to represent the orientation of the surface. Normals behave slightly differently to ordinary vectors when certain operations are performed on them, and the compiler may also use this information to detect potential errors in your code. Old implementations of RenderMan simply used the type "point" for all vectors, and this is still reflected in some documentation but in modern code "point" should only be used to represent a position in space.

Depending on your implementation, you may have to declare all variables at the beginning of your code (as in C) or you may be able to declare variables immediately before you need them (as in C++). While the former style is more portable, inline declarations can make short examples more readable. Should your compiler have problems, simply separate the declaration and move it to the top of the shader code:

```
normal Nf;
...
Nf=faceforwards(N,I);
```

The variable Nf is given the value of N, flipped (if necessary) so that it is facing toward the observer. However, the length of Nf has no meaning, as we are using it purely to represent the surface's orientation. Therefore, when we use Nf in a shader (Listing 19.2) we also need to scale it so that has a unit length (i.e. it is one unit long). Using normals of nonunit length can generate unpredictable results, so it is important to remember to do this. To confuse matters, scaling a vector so that it has unit length is called normalization, and is implemented in SL by a function called normalize(). Though we often have to normalize normals, the two are completely unrelated and unfortunately just happen to share similar names.

Listing 19.2 A diffuse shader.

```
surface second ()
{
    normal Nf=faceforward (normalize(N),I);
    Oi=Os;
    Ci=Cs * diffuse(Nf) * Oi;
}
```

Collecting Light

In the shader "second" the predefined function diffuse() is included in the calculation of Ci. Diffuse() does all the work of collecting light from sources in the scene and calculating how much is reflected by the surface. It models a rough surface, which scatters light in all directions equally (Figure 19.2). To calculate this, it need to know the surface normal (Nf) but not the observer's position (I), as the value calculated is independent of where the camera is.

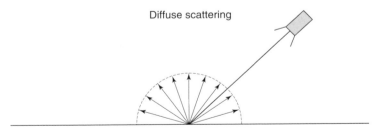

FIGURE 19.2. Diffuse scattering

The value returned by `diffuse()` is not simply the brightness of the lights but also the color. However, one of the benefits of SL over C and other programming languages is that it knows about colors and other variable types used in rendering. It is, therefore, perfectly reasonable to add together or multiply colors, and the results will be correct. The "`second`" shader is very similar to the standard shader "`matte`" which is defined in Listing 19.3. In addition to diffuse lighting, the contribution from any ambient light is included by the call to `ambient()` to ensure that the dark sides of objects are not completely black. The collected light is multiplied by the surface color and by `Oi` then assigned to the output `Ci` to produce a surface which looks like Figure 19.3 (see also Plate II, Figure 12.2).

Listing 19.3 The matte shader.

```
surface matte (
          float Ka=1;
          float Kd=1;
          )
{

    normal Nf=faceforward (normalize(N),I);

    Oi=Os;
    Ci=Oi * Cs * (Ka * ambient() + Kd * diffuse(Nf));
}
```

FIGURE 19.3. The matte shader (see also Plate II, Figure 12.2)

`Matte` also has two parameters "Ka" and "Kd", which control the contributions from diffuse and ambient lighting. These can be assigned by parameter list in the RIB file (and typically in the modeler), allowing the shader's appearance to be modified by an animator without having to modify the code. To create such a parameter you must not only declare the parameters but also provide default value. If no explict value is provided when the shader is applied to an object, then these values will be used.

Metal

`Matte` models a rough surface which scatters light, but real surfaces often reflect light in a more coherent fashion. When you view a metallic surface from the correct angle light will be reflected directly towards you creating a bright "specular" highlight. Depending on the texture of the surface this highlight may be bright and sharply defined, or more evenly spread over a large area. Such reflections are illustrated in Figure 19.4.

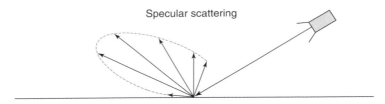

FIGURE 19.4. Specular reflection

This form of reflection is modeled by the function `specular()`. In order to calculate the amount of light being reflected in a particular direction, we will need to tell it the surface normal, the roughness of the surface, and the direction the surface is being viewed from (for which we would like to calculate the reflection).

The direction towards the viewer is typically stored in a variable called V and while unlike Ci, Cs, N and other globals, the use of the name V is purely a convention. The adoption of standard names for commonly used information makes shaders easier to read. Nf is also a commonly adopted name to mean the face forwards surface normal. V is the direction back towards the observer, so we simply add the line:

```
vector V=normalize(-I);
```

as I is the vector *from* the observer to the point on the surface. V is of type vector as it is a free vector with no special properties other than indicating a direction.

In Listing 19.4, in place of `diffuse()`, the function `specular()` has been called, resulting in a highlight which is dependent on the observer's position as well as the position of the light.

FIGURE 11.1. Pointlight

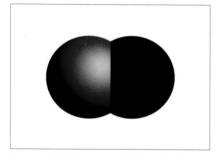

FIGURE 11.2. Turning a light off and on

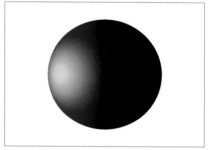

FIGURE 11.3. Distantlight

FIGURE 11.4. Spotlight

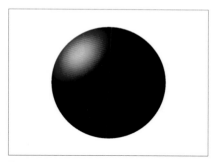

FIGURE 11.6. Softening the edge of a spotlight

FIGURE 11.7. Ambientlight

FIGURE 11.8. Ambient and spotlight

FIGURE 12.1. The "constant" shader

FIGURE 12.2. The "matte" shader

FIGURE 12.3. The "metal" shader

FIGURE 12.5. The "plastic" shader

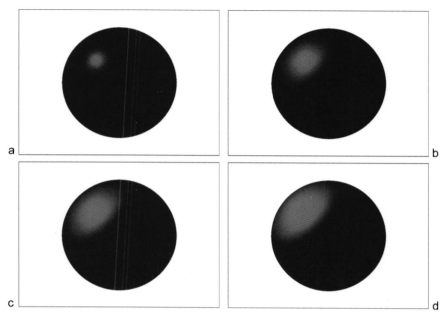

FIGURE 12.4. (**a**) roughness = 0.01 (**b**) roughness = 0.05 (**c**) roughness = 0.1 (**d**) roughness = 0.2

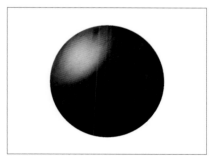

FIGURE 12.6. Using "`plastic`" to stimulate metal

FIGURE 12.9. A displacement shader

FIGURE 12.8. The "`paintedplastic`" shader

Creating bands

A soft edge

A vertical line

Layering two effects

Blending two colors

The HSV color space

A disk

Arbitrary lines

FIGURE 14.2. Scene without shadows

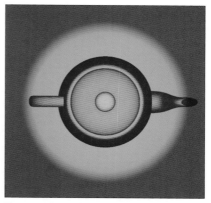

FIGURE 14.3. The scene viewed from the light source

FIGURE 14.5. Scene with shadows

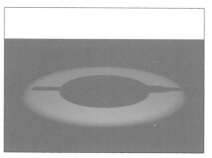

FIGURE 14.6. Shadow without an object

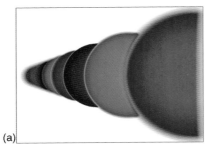
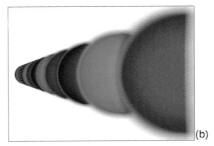

(a)   (b)

FIGURE 15.3. (**a**) A short focal distance of 2m (**b**) A larger focal distance of 5m

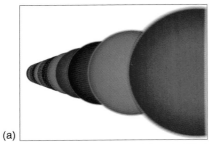

(a)   (b)

FIGURE 15.4. (**a**) A short focal length (**b**) A long focal length

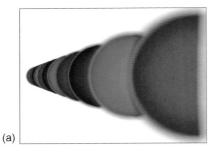
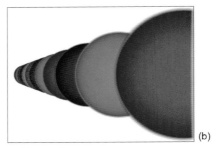

(a)   (b)

FIGURE 15.5. (**a**) A small f-stop value (**b**) A large f-stop value

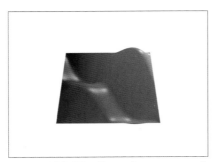

FIGURE 16.2. Blending colors over a surface   FIGURE 17.3. Changing the color of points

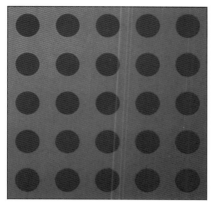

FIGURE 22.2. A repeating pattern

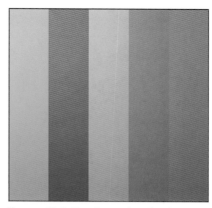

FIGURE 22.5. Random colored stripes

FIGURE 22.6. Random colored tiles

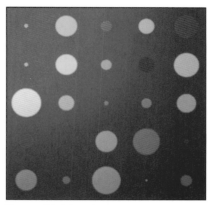

FIGURE 22.7. Random disks

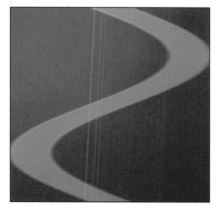

FIGURE 22.8. Deforming the texture coordinates

FIGURE 26.9. Using turbulance with a spline

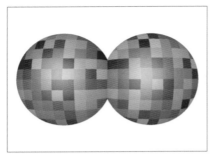

FIGURE 23.1. Orthographic projection

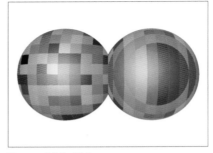

FIGURE 23.2. Object space

FIGURE 23.3. Shader space

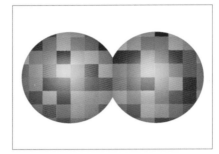

FIGURE 23.4. Perspective projection

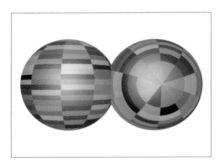

FIGURE 23.5. Cylindrical projection

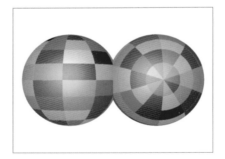

FIGURE 23.6. Spherical projection

FIGURE 23.7. Spheres carved from cubes

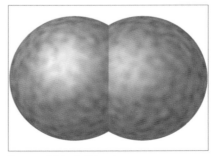

FIGURE 26.3. Solid noise

FIGURE 26.4. Using noise to deform textures

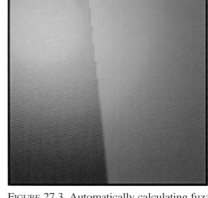

FIGURE 27.3. Automatically calculating fuzz

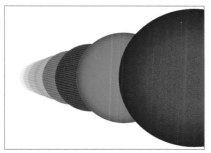

FIGURE 29.1. A simple depth fade

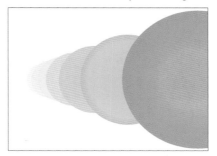

FIGURE 29.2. A fog effect

FIGURE 29.3. A point light

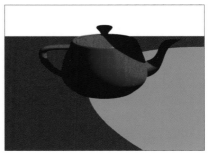

FIGURE 29.4. A Nonphysical light

FIGURE 29.5. A conical beam

FIGURE 29.6. Modifying a lights color

FIGURE 24.9. A reflective surface

FIGURE 28.3. Reorienting the satin shader

FIGURE 30.1. Ray-traced shadows

FIGURE 30.2. Ray-traced reflections

FIGURE 30.3. Tracing multiple rays

FIGURE 30.4. Bounced light

FIGURE 30.5. Indirect diffuse illumination

FIGURE 30.6. Caustics

South African wines, rendered with RenderDrive. © Theseus Projects.
(Courtesy of Advanced Rendering Technology.)

Aircraft interior, rendered with RenderDrive. © Bombadier Aerospace Inc.
(Courtesy of Advanced Rendering Technology.)

"Mr. Finnegan's Giving Chest" rendered with 3Delight. ©DAZ Productions, Inc.

"Mr. Finnegan's Giving Chest" rendered with 3Delight. ©DAZ Productions, Inc.

"Tugboat II" rendered with Aqsis. © Vikram Mulligan

"Fur" rendered as 758,019 individual curves. RIB data provided by Joe Alter, Inc
(www.joealter.com). Rendered with RenderDotC

Flowers, rendered with Air (image courtesy of Haggi Flöser).

Listing 19.4 A specular shader.

```
surface third ()
{
    normal Nf=faceforward (normalize(N),I);
    vector V=-normalize(I);

    Oi=Os;
    Ci=Oi * Cs * specular(Nf,V,0.1);
}
```

This shader models the appearance of a rough metal surface, and is closely related to the standard RenderMan shader "metal" which is listed in Listing 19.5. Once again the standard version adds an ambient contribution, along with controls to let an end user modify the surface. The resulting image is shown in Figure 19.5 (see also Plate II, Figure 12.3).

Listing 19.5 The metal shader.

```
surface metal (
        float Ka=1;
        float Ks=1;
        float roughness=.1;)
{
    normal Nf=faceforward (normalize(N),I);
    vector V=-normalize(I);

    Oi=Os;
    Ci=Oi * Cs *
        (Ka*ambient()+Ks*specular(Nf,V,roughness));
}
```

FIGURE 19.5. The metal shader (see also Plate II, Figure 12.3)

Plastic

In practice, most surfaces combine some degree of both a diffuse and a specular highlight as in Figure 19.6 (see also Plate II, Figure 12.5). This was produced using the standard shader "plastic" shown in Listing 19.6, which combines the functionality of both matte and metal.

Listing 19.6 The plastic shader.

```
surface plastic (
        float Ka=1;
        float Kd=.5;
        float Ks=.5;
        float roughness=.1;
        color specularcolor=1;)
{
    normal Nf=faceforward (normalize(N),I);
    vector V=-normalize(I);

    Oi=Os;
    Ci=Oi * ( Cs * (Ka*ambient()+Kd*diffuse(Nf))
    +specularcolor * Ks*specular(Nf,V,roughness)
    );
}
```

FIGURE 19.6. The plastic shader (see also Plate II, Figure 12.5)

In the plastic shader the RIB color Cs is used to control the color of the diffuse lighting, while the color of the specular highlight is controlled by the parameter specularcolor. This models plastic relatively well for reasons discussed in Chapter 12. By adjusting the weighting parameters (Ka, Kd, and Ks) and changing specularcolor, however, it is possible to reproduce any of the effects of matte or metal. For this reason plastic forms a good starting point from which more complex shaders can be developed.

Summary

`Cs`

The surface color declared in the RIB file.

`Os`

The opacity color declared in the RIB file.

`Ci`

The final surface color calculated by the shader.

`Oi`

The final surface opacity calculated by the shader.

`N`

The surface normal.

`Nf`

The face forward surface normal.

`I`

A vector from the camera to the surface.

`V`

The direction of the camera from the surface.

`faceforward(N,I)`

Calculates a vector parallel to *N*, but facing forwards when viewed along *I*.

`normalize(N)`

Calculates a vector of unit length with the same orientation as *N*.

`diffuse(N)`

Calculates diffuse lighting for the surface.

`specular(N,V,roughness)`

Calculates specular lighting for the surface.

Related Functions

phong(N,V,size)

Though it is little used, SL also supports the Phong shading model, which behaves much like specular. The choice is an aesthetic one, but specular() is usually preferred.

Chapter 20
Color Ramps

Introduction

Having established a basic technique for lighting our object we can now move on
to the task of creating variations across the surface. In this chapter we introduce
the most basic of such variations—a ramp of color changing smoothly from one
side of the object to the other.

A Standard Shader

Though the whole process of calculating the color of a surface point is referred to
as shading, and in RenderMan any custom code written in SL is known as a
shader, the term shading more strictly refers to the calculation of the interaction
of light with the surface. Though a little clichéd the standard plastic model provides reasonable flexibility when used intelligently and (at least in the short-term)
we can consider the actual shading part of our shader done. In fact what most
shaders are concerned with is the *variation* of properties such as color and roughness, across the surface—variation which we will refer to as texturing. It is these
variations which create visual interest, and make rendered images spring to life
rather than appearing dull and artificial.

   If you consider the plastic model as a black box, then each of the variables
it uses (`Ka`, `Kd`, `Ks`, `Cs`, `Os`, `specularcolor`, `Nf`, `V`, and `roughness`) is an
input while the variables `Ci` and `Oi` are its outputs. In the standard shaders most
of the input variables are constant across the whole surface but we can manipulate any of them to create a more realistic image. At the very least you would
expect a surface to have some variation in color. Based on this premise, we can
create a standard shader that we can use as a template for further shader development. Such a starting point is shown in Listing 20.1.

Listing 20.1 A standard shader template.

```
surface standard (
        float Ka=1;
        float Kd=.5;
        float Ks=.5;
        float roughness=.1;
        color specularcolor=1;)
{
    /*Initialization*/
    normal Nf=faceforward (normalize(N),I);
    vector V=-normalize(I);
    color Ct;

    /*Texturing*/
    Ct=Cs;

    /*Shading*/
    Oi=Os;
    Ci=Oi * ( Ct * (Ka*ambient()+Kd*diffuse(Nf))+
        specularcolor * Ks*specular(Nf,V,roughness)));
}
```

This is functionally identical to plastic, but it has now been broken into three sections: initialization, where V and Nf are set up; texturing, where we calculate a new variable Ct — the color of the textured surface; and shading, where Ct is used in the plastic shading model. In our standard shader the textured surface color Ct is simply assigned the value of Cs, but it is this texturing part of the shader we will be developing further.

We generally will not specify the whole shader in future, but simply the texturing section, as the shading and setup sections would not be changing in most of our examples. When a code fragment results in the calculation of Ct, it will be assumed that the code should be placed into the standard shader.

A Simple Ramp

Perhaps the simplest texture we could have is a ramp, where the texture changes color smoothly across the surface. To do this you need to know where on the surface you currently are, and this information is provided by two variables, u and v, which tell us how far across and how far up the surface we are. Both range from 0 at the bottom left to 1 at the top right. This works for most of the RenderMan geometry types because they are based on patches — that is, they have four corners.

Although a sphere may not appear to have corners, you can unwrap the surface like a world map from a globe. Each point in the world can uniquely be identified by a set of two-dimensional coordinates, u being longitude and v being latitude. Using the same approach we can take a rectangular image and wrap it onto a sphere to in a simple, unambiguous fashion. This technique also works for all the other quadrics and patches (including NURBS).

Unfortunately such a neat mapping from u/v to a position on the object is not possible in the case of polygons, and this is one of the reasons their use is discouraged. Polygons do have u/v coordinates but they generally do not work very well. However, as the techniques required to get round this problem are a little more complex, we will defer the subject for a later section.

You could use the variables u and v to calculate a value for Ct, but there is a slightly better way: RenderMan provides a second set of two-dimensional coordinates s and t, which by default are identical to u and v. The difference is that s and t can be modified by the modeler, if the end user wishes to change the position of the texture. While u and v always refer to the underlying geometry, s and t refer to how the user wishes the surface to be textured. Generally you should use s and t when evaluating textures, and if the user does not change them then we are back to uv anyway. As s and t provide us with our position in texture space, a ramp shader can be as simple as:

```
Ct = s;
```

which creates a ramp from black on the left to white on the right (Figure 20.1).

FIGURE 20.1. A horizontal ramp (s)

Alternatively:

```
Ct = t;
```

creates the vertical ramp shown in Figure 20.2. For clarity, these have been rendered on a simple tile which makes the texture coordinates obvious.

FIGURE 20.2. A vertical ramp (*t*)

If you are from a programming background you might notice that something strange is going on. S is a scaler, that is, it contains a single value, which in this case ranges from 0 at the left, to 1 on the right, yet Ct is a color which typically requires three components to specify the red, green and blue intensities. Most programming languages would consider assigning a scaler to an array to be an error of some sort, but SL is specifically designed to handle this sort of situation. SL knows that Ct is a color, but it also knows that a scaler value such as s can represent a grayscale value—an intensity. Assigning s to Ct therefore converts 0 to black, 1 to white and similarly for shades of gray in between, producing the desired ramp.

The ramps blend from black on the left (bottom) to white on the right (top). To make the ramp to go the other way (from right to left) you could replace s with 1-s. Where s=0 then 1-s=1, and when s=1 then 1-s=0, so the locations of black and white are reversed, as in Figure 20.3.

FIGURE 20.3. Reversing the ramp $(1-s)$

A Colored Ramp

If you want to convert the grayscale ramp into a colored ramp you need to multiply the intensity by a color, and since the user has provided us with Cs, it is probably best to use that (though we are under no obligation). To produce a horizontal ramp we simply assign

```
Ct=s*Cs;
```

A similar vertical ramp could be generated using

```
Ct=t*Cs;
```

Once again the shading language knows intensities can be combined with colors to produce colors of varying brightness.

If we could create a left–right ramp of one color, and a right–left ramp of a second color then adding them together would produce a blend between the two colors—the original colors are found at each edge and as one fades to black the other would fade in.

As this requires two colors we will specify the second with an expression:

```
color "rgb" (0,1,0);
```

This creates bright green. Note that in addition to providing the three component values of the color, we have specified that these should be treated as an rgb value. Other color spaces can be used to good effect, as in Plate IV (the HSV color space). The code in Listing 20.2 produces this image by simply using s to specify the hue, and t to specify the saturation.

Listing 20.2 The HSV color space.

```
Ct=color "hsv" (s,t,1);
```

Having chosen the two colors to use we simply create a left–right ramp of green, a right–left ramp of the Cs, and add them together, as in Listing 20.3.

Listing 20.3 A color blend.

```
color green;
green=color "rgb" (0,1,0);
    Ct=(1-s)*Cs+s*green;
```

However, this mixing operation is so common that a standard function is provided to do it. Mix() takes two colors and blends them together based upon the third parameter, as demonstrated in Listing 20.4. The results of the two shaders (Plate IV, Blending two colors) in blending two colors are identical, though the code of Listing 20.4 is slightly clearer.

Listing 20.4 Using mix.

```
color green;
green=color "rgb" (0,1,0);
Ct=mix(Cs,green,s);
```

Generalizing the Shader

Having arrived at an effect that you are happy with, the time comes to release the shader into general use. However, before doing so, we should consider if we could make it a little more flexible. During development it made perfect sense to produce a green ramp from left to right, but once in use it would be frustrating to have to keep modifying the shader or maintain multiple copies each almost identical if a slightly different effect was needed.

The most obvious limitation of the shader is that the user may want to choose their own color. We should, therefore, probably replace the variable green with a parameter, allowing the blend color to be easily changed. Typically you should examine your shader for any constants that may need to be changed, and make these into parameters. However, you should also be cautious of making the shader too flexible—it is far simpler to have a number of shaders each creating one type of surface, than to have an incredibly complex shader with hundreds of parameters.

We might also choose to allow the user to select between a horizontal or vertical ramp. The completed shader including the standard template is shown in Listing 20.5.

Listing 20.5 A general ramp.

```
surface ramp (
        color otherColor = color "rgb" (0,1,0);
        float orientation = 0;
        float Ka=1;
        float Kd=.5;
        float Ks=.5;
        float roughness=.1;
        color specularcolor=1;)
{
    normal Nf=faceforward (normalize(N),I);
    vector V=-normalize(I);
    color Ct;

    if(orientation=0)
        Ct=mix(Cs,otherColor,s);
    else
        Ct=mix(Cs,otherColor,t);

    Oi=Os;
    Ci=Oi * ( Ct * (Ka*ambient()+Kd*diffuse(Nf))+
        specularcolor * Ks*specular(Nf,V,roughness));
}
```

Remember that though the standard shader template only varies the color, you can use ramps to modify any part of the shading code. For example, you could create a surface which is more opaque at one side by adding a variable Ot, assigning a ramp to it, and using it in place of Os in the lighting model.

Summary

u,v

Surface coordinates, which define a position upon the surface being shaded.

s,t

Texture coordinates, which define how a surface has been texture mapped in the modelling package. By default these are the same as u,v.

```
color "rgb"  (r,g,b);
color "hsv"  (h,s,v);
```

These specify colors within the code. Colors are usually specified by three parameters, but these can have different interpretations depending on the colorspace used. RGB, and HSV are the most common spaces, but others may also be defined depending upon your renderer.

```
mix(col1, col2, blendval);
```

Mix blends between two colors. If blendval is 0 then the result is col1. If blendval is 1 then col2 is returned.

Chapter 21
Simple Patterns

Introduction

Having learnt that s and t can be used to specify points on the surface of objects, we will now look at how these coordinates can be used to draw patterns upon the surface. While these shapes will be quite simple, we can combine them together with more complex results.

Bands

After ramps, the next simplest pattern you could draw on a surface would be to divide it into two regions based on one of the texture coordinates—for example, to make the top red, and the bottom green as in Plate IV. To do this we can use the variable t to decide if we are in the top or bottom half of the object, and assign colors to Ct accordingly. The code to do this is in Listing 21.1.

Listing 21.1 Creating bands.

```
color red=color "rgb" (1,0,0);
color green=color "rgb" (0,1,0);
if(t<0.5)
    Ct=green
else
    Ct=red;
```

While this works, it creates a very sharp transition—a point is either completely red or completely green. In a single still frame this is not a problem, but in an animation pixels would "pop" from one side to the other. This is just one instance of a more general problem known is aliasing, which will be discussed in greater depth in Chapter 27. In general if statements should be used with caution in shaders.

To avoid such a sharp edge, the transition from top to bottom needs to be smoothed so that points on the border are somewhere between red and green. This is done using the function smoothstep(), which is plotted in Figure 21.1. Smoothstep takes two parameters that represent the start and the end of a transition, while a third parameter represents the position we are testing.

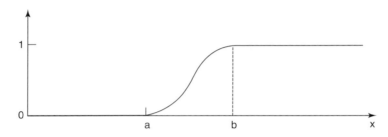

FIGURE 21.1. Smoothstep(a, b, x).

A revised shader based on smoothstep() is shown in Listing 21.2. If t is less than 0.4 then the result of smoothstep() will be 0, while inTop will be assigned 1 if t is greater than 0.6. Between these values the value returned by smoothstep() will change gradually, avoiding any sharp transitions such as those produced by an if statement which either selects red or green. The value inTop is then used to mix between red and green, to produce a soft edge, which avoids popping, as in Plate IV.

Listing 21.2 A soft edge.

```
float inTop;
color red=color "rgb" (1,0,0);
color green=color "rgb" (0,1,0);

inTop=smoothstep(0.4,0.6,t);
Ct=mix(green,red,inTop);
```

We can consider this kind of code as a sort of fuzzy logic. As in regular logic 1 means true—the point is in the top region, while 0 means false—the point is not in the top region. However, some points are somewhere in between, so the variable inTop can also hold values somewhere between true and false.

Lines

To produce a line vertically down the centre of the object you would first need to find the distance of the point being shaded from the centre:

```
float dist=abs(s-0.5).
```

At the centre s is 0.5 so by subtracting 0.5 from s we can find out how far we are from there. We use the function `abs()` to throw away the sign of the result, as we do not care which side of the line the point is on.

If we decide the line is to be 0.2 wide then points a distance of less than 0.1 on either side of the centre will be inside the line. Once again you should use `smoothstep()` to soften the lines edge, as in Listing 21.3. We have used a variable `fuzz` to specify the softness of the edge, rather than adjusting the boundaries explicitly. However, `smoothstep()` will return 1 if the distance is *greater* than $0.1+\text{fuzz}$, so we use $1-\text{smoothstep}()$ making the result 1 (true) inside the line, and zero (false) outside the line. The variable `inLine` is finally used to mix between red and green to produce the green line on a red background seen in Plate IV.

Listing 21.3 A vertical line.

```
color red=color "rgb" (1,0,0);
color green=color "rgb" (0,1,0);
float fuzz=0.025;

float dist=abs(s-0.5);
float inLine=1-smoothstep(0.1-fuzz,0.1+fuzz,dist);

Ct=mix(red,green,inLine);
```

We could combine this line with the previous top/bottom split example to produce a blue line on a red and green background, seen in Plate IV, by mixing the blue line over the old background (Listing 21.4). We first set `Ct` to be green, and then layer red over it if the point is "`inTop`." The result is stored in `Ct` and carried forward to the next calculation which mixes between this color and blue depending on to the extent that the point is "`inLine`." This kind of layering allows patterns of increasing complexity to be built up gradually from simple elements.

Listing 21.4 Layering two effects.

```
float fuzz=0.025;
float inTop;
float inLine;
float dist;
Ct=green;
inTop=smoothstep(0.5-fuzz,0.5+fuzz,t);
Ct=mix(Ct,red,inTop);

dist=abs(s-0.5);
inLine=1-smoothstep(0.1-fuzz,0.1+fuzz,dist);
Ct=mix(Ct,blue,inLine);
```

Circles

You can use the same approach to create a disk of color (see Plate IV). We need to find the distance of the point being shaded from the center of the disk, and then decide if that point is inside or outside the shape. If we center the disk at 0.5,0.5 then using Pythagoras, the distance from the centre to the current point is:

```
float dist=sqrt((s-0.5)*(s-0.5)+(t-0.5)*(t-0.5));
```

We can simply drop this into our previous code, testing this distance to see if we are inside the disk, and then using the result to layer a new color over the existing value of Ct, as in Listing 21.5. For increased flexibility we have set the background color to Cs — as specified by the modeler.

Listing 21.5 A disk.

```
color blue=color "rgb" (0,0,1);
float fuzz=0.025;
float dist;
float inDisk;

Ct=Cs;

dist=sqrt((s-0.5)*(s-0.5)+(t-0.5)*(t-0.5));
inDisk=1-smoothstep(0.3-fuzz,0.3+fuzz,dist);
Ct=mix(Ct,blue,inDisk);
```

As an alternative to calculating the distance ourselves we could use the function `distance()`. This calculates the distance between two points in three-dimensional space. The only complication is that we need to turn our two-dimensional texture coordinates into three dimensional-points before we can use them with `distance()`. This is done as shown in Listing 21.6. Though it may

Listing 21.6 Using the distance () function.

```
float dist;
float inDisk;
point centre=point (0.5,0.5,0);
point here=point (s,t,0);

Ct=Cs;

dist=distance(centre,here);
inDisk=1-smoothstep(0.3-fuzz,0.3+fuzz,dist);
Ct=mix(Ct,blue,inDisk);
```

appear as if we are calling a function called "point," infact we are just assembling the three coordinates into a point, rather like we do when specifying a color.

The results from either approach are identical, though the second is probably slightly clearer.

More Lines

The lines we have drawn so far have been limited to being vertical or horizontal. To define arbitrary lines as in Plate IV you need to specify a start and an end point. The maths to calculate the distance of a point from a line is slightly more complex, but fortunately it is handled for us by the built-in function ptlined(). Given a start point, an end point, and the point to consider, it will return the required distance which we can then use in the standard fashion (Listing 21.7).

Listing 21.7 Using the ptlined function.

```
float fuzz=0.025;
float dist;
float inLine;
point start=point (0.1,0.3,0);
point end=point (0.7,0.7,0);
point here=point(s,t,0);

Ct=Cs;

dist=ptlined(start,end,here);
inLine=1-smoothstep(0.1-fuzz,0.1+fuzz,dist);
Ct=mix(Ct,blue,inLine);
```

Boolean Operations

In addition to layering patterns you can combine them, to find parts of the object which are inside or outside one pattern, and also inside or outside another. Given two shapes A and B, for which you have calculated the variables: `inA` and `inB` then

`1-inA`	The point is outside A
`inA*inB`	The point is inside A and B
`inA*(1-inB)`	The point is inside A but outside B
`(1-inA)*(1-inB)`	The point is outside A and B
`1-(1-inA)*(1-inB)`	The point is inside A or it is inside B

Summary

```
float smoothstep(float start, float end,
                 float here)
```
If `here` is less than `start` then the result is 0. If it's more than `end` then the result is 1. If `here` lies somewhere between then the value returned varies smoothly.

```
float mix(color c1, color c2, float blend)
```
Mixes between `c1` and `c2` depending on the value of `blend`.

```
float distance(point p1, point p1)
```
Calculates the distance between the points `p1` and `p2` in 3D space.

```
float ptlined(point start, point end, point here);
```
Calculates the distance from the point `here` to the line from `start` to `end`.

Chapter 22
Tiling and Repeating Patterns

Introduction

In this chapter, we will see how the simple patterns we created in the earlier chapter can be duplicated across a surface to create a more complex pattern. We will use pseudorandom numbers to modify the pattern upon each repetition to add visual interest to the texture.

Creating Tiles

As all our patterns are based on the texture coordinates (s, t) we can manipulate these prior to the generation of the basic motif to produce a more complex overall effect. If the texture coordinates repeat, so will the pattern. The standard texture coordinates s and t cannot be changed, so we will use two new variables, ss and tt to store these modified coordinates.

To duplicate a pattern horizontally five times, we simply multiply s by five (so it ranges from zero to five), then throw away the whole number part. This creates a new texture coordinate that goes from zero to one five times rather than once (Figure 22.1). We remove the integer part of a number using the mod() function which divides the first number by the second and returns the remainder. For example mod(3.7,1) divides 3.7 by 1 which goes three times with 0.7 left over.

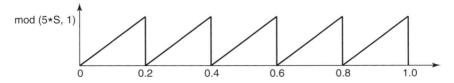

FIGURE 22.1. ss=mod (s*5,1)

The modified texture coordinates are stored in `ss` (and `tt`) and then simply used to replace `s` and `t` throughout the rest of the texture. In Listing 22.1 we have used `ss` and `tt` in place of `s` and `t` in the disk texture from the earlier chapter. The result shown in Figure 22.2 (also Plate VII), is a repeating pattern over the surface.

Listing 22.1 A repeating pattern.

```
float fuzz=0.025;
float dist;
float inDisk;
float ss=mod(s*5,1);
float tt=mod(t*5,1);
point centre=point (0.5,0.5,0);
point here=point (ss,tt,0);

Ct=Cs;

dist=distance(centre,here);
inDisk=1-smoothstep(0.3-fuzz,0.3+fuzz,dist);
Ct=mix(Ct,blue,inDisk);
```

FIGURE 22.2. A repeating pattern (also Plate VII)

Identifying Tiles

To make this pattern more interesting we probably want to modify the basic motif so that it is slightly different in each cell. To do this you need to know which cell we are in as well as the position in the cell. Where we used the `mod()` function to obtain the fractional part of a number we can use `floor()` to obtain the integer part, as in Listing 22.2 and Figure 22.3. Here we have multiplied s by five, and then taken the integer part to obtain five distinct regions. We can then use the variable `which-stripe` to modify the surface. However, as this is constant over each region it will create stripes within the texture. In this case we have used `mod(whichStripe,2)` which divides `whichStripe` by 2, leaving a remainder of either 0 or 1. As a result odd stripes are colored white while even stripes are black.

Listing 22.2 Creating stripes.

```
float repeatCount=5;
float whichStripe=floor(s*repeatCount);
Ct=mod(whichStripe,2);
```

FIGURE 22.3. Creating stripes

By applying this idea to both the s and t directions you can create a set of tiles where each square is modified depending upon its position on the surface. We have done this in Listing 22.3. By simply adding together the stile and ttile values we create the checkerboard seen in Figure 22.4. Where the sum is odd we generate a white square, while an even sum results in a black square.

Listing 22.3 Creating tiles.

```
float repeatCount=5;
float sTile=floor(s*repeatCount);
float tTile=floor(t*repeatCount);
Ct=mod(sTile+tTile,2);
```

FIGURE 22.4. Creating tiles

Though this does works it has the kind of sharp edges that you should use smoothstep() to avoid and will look very bad when viewed from too far a way. We will construct a better checkerboard in Chapter 27, when we look at the problem of aliasing in greater detail.

CellNoise

Having established which tile we are shading, the next step is to generate a random value for that cell. We do not want the result to be truly random, however. In fact, we want it to be repeatable between renders and consistent over the entire tile. This is the purpose of the `cellnoise()` function. This takes a number, throws away the fractional part to obtain the tile number and then returns a pseudo random number based upon that value. The important thing about this operation is that it will consistently return the same value for the whole cell. Listing 22.4 uses `cellnoise()` to generate the random colored stripes seen in Figure 22.5 (also Plate VII).

Listing 22.4 Random colored stripes.

```
float repeatCount=5;
float ss=s*repeatCount;
Ct=color cellnoise(ss);
```

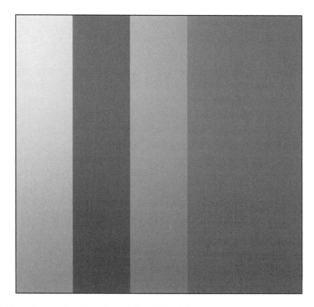

FIGURE 22.5. Random colored stripes (also Plate VII)

If you wanted to allocate colors in a grid, to create a randomly colored set of tiles like Figure 22.6 (also Plate VII), then we could pass values based on both s and t coordinates to `cellnoise()`. This is demonstrated in Listing 22.5.

Listing 22.5 Random colored tiles.

```
float repeatCount=5;
float ss=s*repeatCount;
float tt=t*repeatCount;
Ct=color cellnoise(ss,tt);
```

FIGURE 22.6. Random colored tiles (also Plate VII)

Like many functions in SL `cellnoise()` can take a varying number of parameters (one float, two floats, one point, or a point and a float). RenderMan will automatically use the right version. Even more flexibly `cellnoise()` can generate either a single number (between 0 and 1), a color or a vector of some kind. While RenderMan may be able to guess what kind of value it is expected to return, there is a good chance it may guess incorrectly, so you should always give RenderMan a hint by prefixing `cellnoise()` with the required type.

In Listing 22.6 we use `cellnoise()` to generate both a random color and a random radius for a tiled set of disk. The radius of each disk is generated by a `float cellnoise()` function. As this normally returns a value of between 0 and 1 we have scaled it by 0.4 to ensure the disk fits within the cell. The color of the disk uses `color cellnoise()` as we've done previously. The result (Figure 22.7, also Plate VII) is a texture that never repeats, and could easily be used on a large number of objects, and yet make each object appear different.

Listing 22.6 Random disks.

```
float repeatCount=5;
float ss=mod(repeatCount*s,1);
float tt=mod(repeatCount*t,1);

point centre=point (0.5,0.5,0);
point here=point (ss,tt,0);
float dist=distance(centre,here);

float radius=float cellnoise(repeatCount*s,
            repeatCount*t)*0.4;
color myColor=color cellnoise(repeatCount*s,
            repeatCount*t);
float inDisk=1-smoothstep(radius-fuzz,radius+fuzz,dist);

Ct=mix(Cs,myColor,inDisk);
```

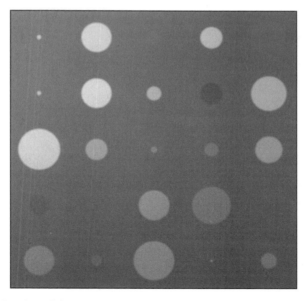

FIGURE 22.7. Random disks (also Plate VII)

Of course there is no reason why every layer of your texture should be tiled the same way. `ss` and `tt` could be generated several times in a single shader using different values of `repeatCount`.

Other Modifications to ss and tt

Though tiling is very common in shaders it is certainly not the only way you can modify the texture coordinates. `ss` and `tt` can be generated in any fashion to scale, rotate or distort the basic pattern. For example, in Listing 22.7 we have added a sine wave to the `s` coordinate, before using the result in texture that would normally produce a vertical line. By using the deformed texture coordinates we get the wavy line in Figure 22.8 (also Plate VII) which is visually far more interesting.

Listing 22.7 Deforming the texture coordinates.

```
float ss=s+sin(t*2*PI)*0.4;
float dist=abs(ss-0.5);
float inLine=1-smoothstep(0.1-fuzz,0.1+fuzz,dist);
Ct=mix(Cs,green,inLine);
```

FIGURE 22.8. Deforming the texture coordinates (also Plate VII)

Summary

```
ss=mod(s*numberOfTiles,1);
whichTileS=floor(s*numberOfTiles);
```
mod and floor can be used to find the fractional and whole part of a number. By scaling s and t these divide the surface into tiles.

```
x=float cellnoise(s);
x=float cellnoise(s,t);
Ct=color cellnoise(s);
Ct=color cellnoise(s,t);
```
Cellnoise calculates a pseudo random value (usually either a single number or a color). Its parameters are rounded down to the nearest whole number, and then used in the calculation, so that areas of the surface will produce the same result.

Chapter 23
Projections and Coordinate Spaces

Introduction

In this chapter, we will see how you can use the position of points in 3D space to texture surfaces. This allows you to create objects that appear to be carved from blocks, and to texture objects for which texture coordinates are inadequate.

3D Coordinates

While s and t are simple and convenient, it is not always possible or appropriate to use them. Patches have well-defined surface coordinates, but other forms of geometry such as polygons, subdivision surfaces and blobby objects cannot be mapped so easily. Even when patches are being used it can be difficult to create seamless textures when an object is constructed from more than one patch. In these cases we need to find other ways of identifying where we are in the texture.

Regardless of the type of surface, you can always identify each point to be shaded by its position in 3D space. This is stored in the global variable P. It is therefore always possible to base the surface color calculation upon this value. You could, for example, simply take the x and y positions, and use those to calculate texturing as in Listing 23.1 and Figure 23.1 (also Plate VIII). This is an orthographic projection, as the texture is projected along the z-axis. The components of a point (or vector) are extracted using the functions xcomp(), ycomp(), and zcomp(). In this case we have used the new texture coordinates, ss and tt, as parameters to cellnoise(), which allows us to see how the texture wraps around the object. However, you could use these coordinates as the basis for any of the effects so far explored.

Listing 23.1 Orthographic projection.

```
float repeatCount=5;
float ss=xcomp(P)*repeatCount;
float tt=ycomp(P)*repeatCount;
Ct=color cellnoise(ss,tt);
```

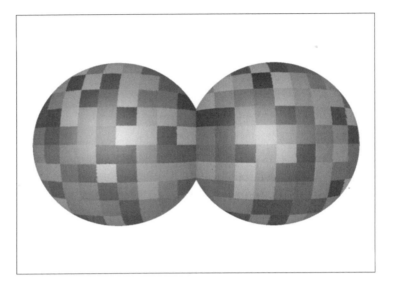

FIGURE 23.1. Orthographic projection (also Plate VIII)

Coordinate Systems

Though P specifies a point in 3D space it is undefined *which* space it is in. Without knowing the location of the origin, and orientation of the axes, we cannot assign any useful meaning to P. If we were shading a sphere we might reasonably like to consider P as being relative to the centre of the sphere. However, transformations are applied to each object to position it relative to the rest of the objects in the world. The world itself is defined relative to the camera's position. P might define the point we are shading relative to the object it is part of, relative to the world, relative to the camera or relative to some totally different frame of reference.

In fact P is defined as being in "current" space—a coordinate system selected by the renderer that is undefined by the RenderMan standard. Different renderers may choose whichever space is easiest for them to perform their calculations in. Figure 23.1 was created in a renderer in which "current" space is equivalent to "camera"—a space with the origin at the camera, looking down the *z*-axis, but given that "current" space is renderer dependent it is clearly foolish to rely on it when applying textures. A different renderer might produce a very different image. Rather than relying on the renderer's choice of coordinate system, you should always transform the point P into a specific frame of reference.

In Listing 23.2 we have created a similar shader to the one used previously, but this time specified that the calculations should be done relative to the position of the object. This is done by transforming the position of P into "object" space, and assigning it to the new variable PP. As PP is in a well-defined coordinate system it can be used for the rest of the calculation with reliable results. Again we have used a convention of PP being some modified version of the variable P.

Listing 23.2 Object space.

```
point PP=transform("object",P);
float repeatCount=5;
float ss=xcomp(PP)*repeatCount;
float tt=ycomp(PP)*repeatCount;
Ct=color cellnoise(ss,tt);
```

When this new shader is applied to the scene we previously shaded in "current" space we get the image in Figure 23.2 (also Plate VIII). The spheres are shaded relative to the coordinate system in which they were created, rather than the position in which they occupy relative to the camera. You can now see that the sphere on the right is in fact rotated, as the squares of color run through it from top to bottom rather than front to back.

FIGURE 23.2. Object space (also Plate VIII)

If we use "object" space to define the coordinates in a shader, then the texture will move as the object does. As an alternative we could use "world"— the coordinate space that was in place when WorldBegin was called in the RIB file. In this case the object would swim through the texture. Between these two spaces is "shader" space. This is the coodinates sytem in which the shader itself was defined, which we have used in Listing 23.3.

Listing 23.3 Shader space.

```
point PP=transform("shader",P);
float repeatCount=5;
float ss=xcomp(PP)*repeatCount;
float tt=ycomp(PP)*repeatCount;
Ct=color cellnoise(ss,tt);
```

By applying a shader to several objects they will share their shader coordinate system, as in Figure 23.3 (also Plate VIII). Here the shader has been created in a rotated coordinate system, and hence the texture is rotated. Because the objects have been textured in a single space the texture flows smoothly from one object to the next, making it easy to create compound objects from several primitives,

FIGURE 23.3. Shader space (also Plate VIII)

It is also possible to shade in "camera" space, which gives the position of the object relative to the camera. Using this would cause objects to change their appearance as the camera moves which would generally be undesirable, but you can use it to create "intelligent" surfaces which change as you look at them.

If none of these coordinate systems is appropriate, it is also possible to create new named coordinate systems in a RIB file using the command

```
CoordinateSystem "name".
```

You can then refer to this named coordinate system from shaders, just as you can the standard coordinate spaces.

More Complex Projections

When painted or photographed textures are used you often need to project them as if from a single point, rather like a slide projector. This is a perspective transformation, and is achieved by dividing the x and y values by the z depth as in Listing 23.4. This particular shader projects a texture from the camera rather like a traditional front projection system. This matches the way the camera projects back onto the film, and hence the result shown in Figure 23.4 (also Plate VIII) is a different effect to that seen in Figure 23.1, which used an orthographic projection in camera space.

Listing 23.4 Perspective projection.

```
point PP=transform("camera",P);
float repeatCount=20;
float ss=xcomp(PP)/zcomp(PP)*repeatCount;
float tt=ycomp(PP)/zcomp(PP)*repeatCount;
Ct=color cellnoise(ss,tt);;
```

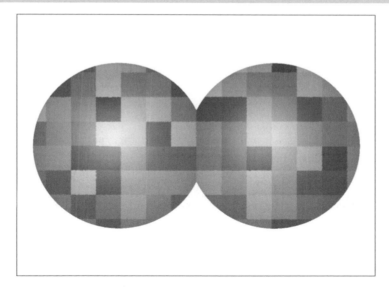

FIGURE 23.4. Perspective projection (also Plate VIII)

For certain objects (such as the heads on characters) the most appropriate projection is a cylindrical one. This takes the *z* coordinate as the t component, and the angle around the axis as the s component. In can be calculated by the code in Listing 23.5. The resulting image in Figure 23.5 (also Plate VIII) is textured as if you had wrapped the texture onto a cylinder, then shrink-wrapped it onto the object.

Listing 23.5 Cylindrical projection.

```
point PP=transform("object",P);
float repeatCount=10;
float ss=atan(xcomp(PP),zcomp(PP))/
          (2*PI)*repeatCount;
float tt=ycomp(PP)*repeatCount;
Ct=color cellnoise(ss,tt);
```

FIGURE 23.5. Cylindrical projection (also Plate VIII)

The other common projection type is spherical, as in Listing 23.6. This textures the object in a similar fashion to the standard st coordinates of a sphere, but may be used for any kind of geometry which is of approximately spherical shape. While ss is as it was for cylindrical projection, the tt coordinates are mapped differently. This is particularly noticeable at the top of the objects, as seen in the right-hand sphere of Figure 23.6 (also Plate VIII), and so you might use it in preference to cylindrical if you needed to look down at the top of a character's head.

Listing 23.6 Spherical projection.

```
float repeatCount=10;
float ss,tt;
vector PP=transform("object",P);
PP=normalize(PP);
ss=(atan(xcomp(PP),zcomp(PP))/(2*PI))*repeatCount;
tt=acos(ycomp(PP))/PI*repeatCount;
Ct=color cellnoise(ss,tt);
```

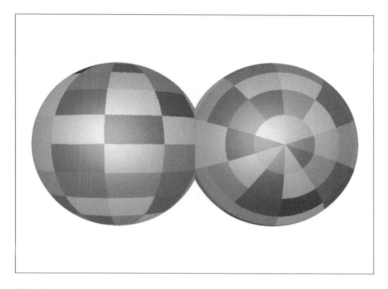

FIGURE 23.6. Spherical projection (also Plate VIII)

Solid Textures

Rather than projecting the point P into two dimensions, and using the 2D coordinates as the basis for texturing, you could skip the projection stage completely, and use the value of P directly to construct a texture. This creates a texture that changes smoothly regardless of how the surface is shaped, and produces an object that appears to have been carved from a solid block of the material. For this reason such textures are generally referred to as solid textures. Extending our tiling examples to three dimensions, you can carve the spheres from cubes of color as in Listing 23.7 and Figure 23.7 (also Plate VIII).

Listing 23.7 Spheres carved from cubes.

```
point PP=transform("object",P);
float repeatCount=5;
Ct=color cellnoise(PP*repeatCount);
```

FIGURE 23.7. Spheres carved from cubes (also Plate VIII)

Solid textures avoid the appearance that a pattern has simply been pasted onto the surface of an object, but rather that it is a real part of the object. We will see how this can be used to create wood and marble effects in Chapter 26.

More Coordinate System Transforms

We have so far assumed that you are transforming a point from the default "current" space to a new coordinate system. However, you might need to transform from this new coodinates system to a third or even back to current. This can be done by passing both "from" and "to" coordinate systems to the transform function. For example:

```
Point origin=transform("camera","object",
                       point (0,0,0));
```

calculates the position of the camera in object space, by transforming the point 0,0,0 from camera space to object space.

You should take care as to exactly what kind of vector we are transforming. So far, only points have been transformed, but surface normals and free vectors may also be transformed between coordinate systems. Different types of vector need to be changed in different ways when converted. `Transform()` is designed to transform points. To make sure that you get the correct type of conversion you should use the functions `vtransform()` and `ntransform()` for vectors and surface normals, respectively.

When writing textures which are based on the 3D position of the surface, it is often useful to allow the end user to choose the coordinate system in which texturing is to be done, so that the completed shader can be used on a wide range of surfaces. This is easily achived by adding a parameter, as in Listing 23.8

Listing 23.8 A space parameter.

```
Surface mySurface ( ....
            string space="world"
            )
    {
    point PP=transform(space,P);
    ...
    }
```

Summary

```
PP=transform([fromspace],tospace,P);
VV=vtransform([fromspace],tospace,V);
NN=ntransform([fromspace],tospace,N);
```
Transform a point, vector and normal respectively from `fromspace` (which defaults to `current`) to `tospace`.

`"object"`
The coordinate system in which the object was created – for example the center of a sphere. Objects may be transformed, but if object space is used then the texture will move with them.

`"shader"`
The space in which the shader was specified in the RIB file.

`"world"`
The coordinate system at `WorldBegin`.

`"camera"`
The coordinate system with the camera at the origin.

Chapter 24
Painted Textures

Introduction

Though writing code is a powerful way of texturing objects, sometimes it is simply easier to paint something by hand then apply that to the object. We are now going to see how that can be done in RenderMan, but more importantly we will look at how painted textures can be combined with procedural textures to give the user the maximum power and control.

Accessing Image Files

Some patterns can be constructed easily using SL code, but for other types of pattern it is clearly easier to paint or photograph the required design, then apply this image to the three-dimensional object. Even in these cases, however, a shader is still required: first to calculate which point on the source image (known as a texture map) corresponds to the surface point being shaded, and then to define how the value from the map will affect the surface.

The most obvious and simplest use of a texture would be to take Ct from the map using the default texture coordinates (s and t). You can do this trivially by using the code in Listing 24.1. The renderer does all the hard work for you, taking into account the file format, and resolution, resizing it automatically to fit the object, to produce an image like Figure 24.1.

Listing 24.1 Applying a texture.

```
Ct=color texture("myTexture.tiff").
```

FIGURE 24.1. Applying a texture

Generally the texture map will be provided by the user of the shader when it is applied in a scene. You should therefore make the name of the map a parameter of the shader, so that it can be specified at render time. In such cases, the shader usually contains code similar to Listing 24.2, which first checks that a file name has been provided, so that if the user chooses not to provide a map, the shader will still operate correctly. In order to simplify the examples in this chapter, however, we will continue to hard code the file names.

Listing 24.2 An optional texture map.

```
surface param ( ...
               string mapname="";
               ...)
    {
    ...
    if(mapname !="")
        Ct=color texture(mapname);
    else
        Ct=Cs;
    ...
    }
```

The textures we will be using are in TIFF format. However, most renderers have a preferred image file format, which has been optimised so texture lookups are as efficient as possible. Before you can use a texture with a particular renderer it usually has to be converted into this format, using a program provided with the renderer.

This should be explained in your renderers documentation. The filename of the converted image should be used in the shader rather than the TIFF filename.

Procedurally Modifying a Texture Map

The `texture` function automatically wraps the texture onto the surface using s and t. As you have learnt, however, simple patterns can be augmented by modifying the texture coordinates before you generate a pattern. In exactly the same way we can calculate new texture coordinate, and ask `texture()` to use these to position the map on the object. In Listing 24.3 we have combined the texture lookup with some standard tiling code to cover the object with copies of the image as shown in Figure 24.2. Combining SL with a texture map gives you total control over texture placement, as you can use any function to generate the texture coordinates. For example, in Listing 24.4 we have added a sine wave to `ss`, and hence deformed the image as in Figure 24.3.

Listing 24.3 Tiling a texture map.

```
float  sRepeatCount=12;
float  tRepeatCount=5;
float  ss=mod(s*sRepeatCount,1);
float  tt=mod(t*tRepeatCount,1);

Ct=color texture("pebbles.tiff",ss,tt);
```

FIGURE 24.2. Tiling a texture map

Listing 24.4 Distorting a texture map.

```
float sRepeatCount=12;
float tRepeatCount=5;
float ss=mod(s*sRepeatCount,1);
float tt=mod(t*tRepeatCount,1);

ss=mod(ss+0.2*sin(t*20),1);

Ct=color texture("pebbles.tiff",ss,tt);
```

FIGURE 24.3. Distorting a texture map

You could even use `cellnoise()` to randomly select between a number of images for each tile, as we have done in Listing 24.5. This combination of coded and painted textures allows you to avoid one of the primary problems of texture maps—that they are always the same. Here we have created a texture which can be applied to as large an area as we require yet will never repeat, as seen in Figure 24.4. Of course these textures do not tile together correctly, and hence the joins are very apparent, but by carefully repainting the texture maps, and using a slightly more complex shader, the results could be convincing.

Listing 24.5 Mixing between texture maps.

```
float sRepeatCount=17;
float tRepeatCount=11;
float ss=s*sRepeatCount;
float tt=t*tRepeatCount;

if(float cellnoise(ss,tt)>0.5)
    Ct=color texture("pebbles.tiff",
                        mod(ss,1),mod(tt,1));
else
    Ct=color texture("rock.tiff",
                        mod(ss,1),mod(tt,1));
```

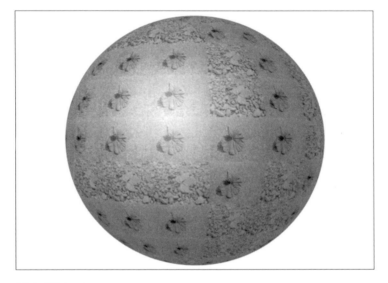

FIGURE 24.4. Mixing between texture maps

Maps as Controls for Procedural Textures

Rather than simply using a texture map as an image that is painted onto the surface and using code to control it, you can also use the painted map to control procedural elements of the shader. Suppose you wish to model a surface that shiny in parts, but matte in other places. Rather than trying to provide parameters to the shader defining which areas are shiny, you could use a texture map to let an artist indicate which areas are specular by simply painting them. In this case, the texture is not being used as a color, but simply as a control. We use "float texture" rather than "color texture" to indicate we want a grayscale value (just as we did with cellnoise).

Such an example is shown in Listing 24.6. The texture map is not used as a color—Ct is constant, but rather the texture map modifies the weighting of specular and diffuse lighting. The resulting image is shown in Figure 24.5.

Listing 24.6 Using a map as a control.

```
float  sRepeatCount=9;
float  tRepeatCount=5;
float  ss=mod(s*sRepeatCount,1);
float  tt=mod(t*tRepeatCount,1);

float  surfaceType=float texture("ShinySurface.tiff",
                                     ss,tt);
Ct=Cs;

Oi=Os;
Ci=Oi  *  ( Ct*(Ka*ambient()+surfaceType*diffuse(Nf))+
        (1-surfaceType)* specular(Nf,V,roughness));
```

FIGURE 24.5. Using a map as a control

Environment Maps

Texture maps accessed by surface coordinates are the simplest and most common form of map, but 2D images may be applied to surfaces in other ways. While most renderers now support ray tracing, it is usually slow. In many cases environment maps can provide a much faster and more flexible alternative. If you are trying to mix CG with live action, you can even use them to create reflections of real objects.

The basic assumption made when using environment maps is that you are rendering a small object in a big world. If we were using ray tracing then a ray from the camera would hit a point on the object's surface, and then a reflected ray would be traced back into the rest of the scene. However, if the object were very small and the environment very big it would not matter very much which point on the surface of the object the reflected ray originated from—we only need to worry about the direction of the reflected ray, as illustrated in Figure 24.6.

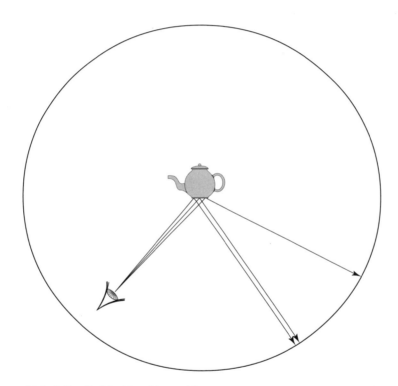

FIGURE 24.6. A Small object in a big world

If we were to photograph or render the scene from the centre of the object and stitched the images together into a panoramic view, then you could extract the color of the environment in any direction from the photograph. Such a photograph is an environment map. Of course, it is only an approximation, as the point being rendered is not actually at the centre of the object. Despite this, it is usually an approximation that is good enough to fool most of the people most of the time.

As we only need to produce one map for the whole object and this map can be reused to render multiple frames, then this is potentially much more efficient than ray tracing.

Generating Environment Maps

When generated by rendering or from photographs, environment maps usually take the form of six square images, one each in the positive and negative x, y, and z directions, forming the six faces of a cube around the object. Such a collection of image is usually displayed as in Figure 24.7. These are stitched together by the `MakeCubeFaceEnvironment` RIB command. This takes the six input files followed by the name of the output file, and a field of view value for the input images. This should generally be a little over 90° so that there are no gaps between the images. The final parameters describe how the image should be filtered: `"gaussian"` 2 2 are appropriate values.

FIGURE 24.7. A cube faced environment Courtesy of Jermome Dewhurst. www.photographica.co.uk

While the cubic form is easy to render and photograph, it does have the disad-
vantage of not being a single image. This makes it hard for artists to work with in
paint packages, and other image manipulation tools. You may prefer to use a
polar form of environment map shown in Figure 24.8. This unwraps the texture
from the surface of a sphere in the same way as a world map is unwrapped from
a globe. Though the whole map is a single image it must still be converted to your
renderer's proprietary format using the RIB command `MakeLongLat-
Environment`. Being simpler than the cubic form this simply requires an input
file, an output file name, and a filter function(`"gaussian" 2 2`). A stand-
alone program to generate environment maps from either cubic or polar images
may also have been supplied with your renderer.

FIGURE 24.8. A polar environment Courtesy of Jermome Dewhurst.
www.photographica.co.uk

Applying Environment Maps

Once converted to the renderer's internal format, we can forget how an environment was generated and concentrate upon using it in our shader. To do this, we
need to first calculate the direction of reflection, and then find the color of the
map in that direction. While it is quite simple to calculate the direction of reflection from the position of the viewer and the orientation of the surface, RenderMan
can to do the work for us. By simply calling the `reflect()` function as in
Listing 24.7, the required direction is calculated. Note that `reflect()` is simply a geometric calculation which works out the *direction* of the new ray, and is
not performing any kind of ray tracing.

Listing 24.7 A reflective surface.

```
surface reflect (
     float Ka=1;
          float Kd=.5;
          float Ks=.4;
          float Kr=.3;
          float roughness=.1;
     color specularcolor=1;)
{
     normal Nf=faceforward (normalize(N),I);
     vector V=-normalize(I);
     color Ct;
     vector Rcurrent=reflect(I,Nf);
     vector Rworld=vtransform("world",Rcurrent);
     color Cr=color environment("studio2.jpg",Rworld);

     Ct=Cs;
     Oi=Os;
     Ci=Oi*(Ct*(Ka*ambient()+Kd*diffuse(Nf))+
          specularcolor*(Ks*specular(Nf, V,roughness)+
          Kr*Cr));
}
```

Once you know the direction of reflection you simply have to pass this, along with the name of the map, to the `environment()` function, and the correct value from the map is returned. However, be sure to convert the direction to an appropriate space (probably `world`), so that the environment map is correctly oriented onto the object. As the value from the environment map represents reflected light we have added it into the plastic shading model with the specular contribution.

The resulting reflections seen in Figure 24.9 (also Plate X) are not physically accurate but will be close enough to fool all but the most critical viewer. Often even a very basic environment map can dramatically increase the realism of objects.

FIGURE 24.9. A reflective surface (also Plate X)

Summary

```
float x=texture("filename" [,ss, tt]);
color c=texture("filename" [,ss,tt]);
```
Read the texture file "filename" at the position ss, tt. The texture coordinates are optional. S, t will be used if none are specified.

```
Vector R=refect(I,N);
```
Calculates the direction R that is the reflection of the vector I in a surface with normal N.

```
float x=environment("filename",R);
color c=environment("filename",R);
```
Read the environment map "filename" in the direction R.

```
MakeCubeFaceEnvironment "px" "nx" "py" "ny" "pz" "nz"
    "envmapname" fov "gaussian" 2 2
MakeLongLatEnvironment "srcmapname"
    "envmapname" "gaussian" 2 2
```
These RIB commands create an environment map called "envmapname." The first takes six images each covering approximately 90° in the positive and negative x, y, and z directions. The second uses a single polar map.

Related Functions

```
vector R=refract(I,N,eta)
```

Refract() calculates the direction of refraction as reflect() does for reflection. Eta is the ratio of the two refractive indices at the surface.

```
fresnel(I,N,eta,Kr,Kt,R,T)
```

Fresnel() calculates both reflection and refraction directions (returned in R and T) along with suggested values as to how these should be weighted when mixed with the rest of the shading calculation (Kr and Kt).

Chapter 25
Displacement

![Introduction heading bar]

Introduction

Shaders can not only change the color and lighting across a surface but can actually change the shape of the surface—a technique known as displacement. This allows you to produce simpler models then fill in surface detail at render time.

![Modifying P heading bar]

Modifying P

In addition to using P (the surface position) to calculate texture coordinates in a surface shader it is also possible to modify P, and in doing so change the shape of the surface. For greater flexibility, and to ease implementation, changing the position of a point on the surface is done in a separate shader to the calculation of surface color. This is known as a "displacement" shader, and is run before the surface shader: the renderer creates a smooth surface, runs the displacement shader to find its final position and orientation, and then runs the surface shader to find its color. This process is shown in Figure 25.1.

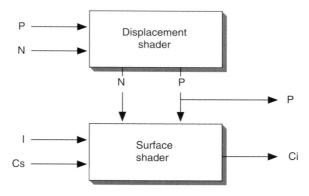

FIGURE 25.1. The displacement process

Officially, the position of a surface should only be modified by a displacement shader but in practice most renderers also allow displacement to be performed in a surface shader. Displacing in a surface shader allows calculations to be performed once, and then used for both displacement and coloring (for example, embossing a colored stripe on a surface), while a separate shader allows a displacement to be mixed with a variety of surface types. In practice, both approaches are used, though we will use displacement shaders, as this is the method that is most portable.

While it is possible to assign any value to P, displacement typically consists of moving the surface in or out a short distance along the surface normal. The displacement shader's job is therefore to calculate the magnitude of this displacement for each point. Most displacement shaders have a structure similar to Listing 25.1.

Listing 25.1 A simple displacement shader.

```
displacement simple (
    float Km=0.1;)
{
    normal NN=normalize(N);
    float mag=0;

    /*Calculate mag*/
    mag=sin(s*10*2*PI)*sin(t*10*2*PI);

    /*Displace*/
    P=P+mag*Km*NN;
    N=calculatenormal(P);
}
```

The surface normal vector can have varying length, so it is first normalized, ensuring its length does not affect the displacement. You can then insert some arbitrary calculation for mag—here we have used a combination of sine waves in s and t. Displacement is performed by adding some multiple of NN to the current position, and assigning it back to the variable P. A parameter to the shader Km provides a control over the total amount of displacement.

Having moved the points of the surface, its curvature will have changed and hence we must recalculate the surface normals (N) by using the function calculatenormal(). Though simple, the combination of shape and lighting produces a remarkably interesting pattern when applied to a sphere as in Figure 25.2.

FIGURE 25.2. A displaced sphere

In the same way that we calculated Ct in the surface shader and then placed that code into a standard framework, for most displacement shaders you simply need to calculate mag. To arrive at a value for mag, you can apply any of the techniques used so far. For example, to emboss a circle onto a surface as in Figure 25.3, we can use the same approach we used to draw a colored circle as in Listing 25.2.

Listing 25.2 Embossing a disk.

```
displacement disk (
    float Km=0.1;)
{

    normal NN=normalize(N);
    float mag=0;
    float fuzz=0.05;

    /*Calculate mag*/
    float dist=sqrt((s-0.5)*(s-0.5)+(t-0.5)*(t-0.5));
    mag=smoothstep(0.3-fuzz,0.3+fuzz,dist);

    /*Displace*/
    P=P+mag*Km*NN;
    N=calculatenormal(P);
}
```

FIGURE 25.3. Embossing a disk

Displacing in the Right Space

While these shaders will operate correctly, their exact behavior is not consistent
between different renderers. As we discussed, earlier, all shading is done in coordinate space known as "current" but the exact meaning of this space is left to
the designer of the renderer. While we know the value of N in "current" space, it
is unclear what the length mag means in any particular space. If "current"
space were equivalent to object space then the displacement would scale with the
object, while if "current" were "camera" space then scaling the object would
leave the displacement unaffected. Figure 25.4 shows a sine wave pattern
embossed onto two spheres—the second sphere being a scaled version of the first.
Unfortunately, because the displacement has been performed in "current"
space the displacement is the same size in both cases, which is unlikely to be the
effect you want.

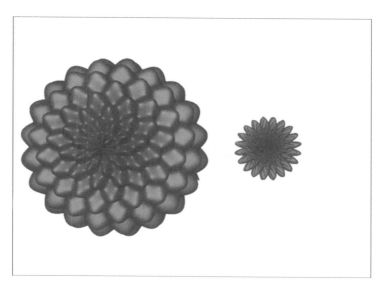

FIGURE 25.4. Displacing in current space

While there is no correct space in which displacement distances should be specified, "object" or "shader" are probably most appropriate, and this can be implemented by including the line:

```
mag /= length(vtransform("object",NN));
```

This scales the displacement by the length of N in object space, and hence mag is now relative to that space. Figure 25.5 shows the effect of adding this to the previous code to produce the shader in Listing 25.3. The displacement has now been scaled, so the two objects correctly appear to be scaled versions of each other. Of course you may choose to displace in other spaces, such as "shader" or "world." For maximum flexibility the displacement space can be specified by a parameter to the shader.

Listing 25.3 Displacing in object space.

```
displacement object (
    float Km=0.1;)
{

    vector NN=normalize(N);
    float mag=0;

    /*Calculate mag*/
    mag=sin(s*10*2*PI) *sin(t*10*2*PI);
    mag /= length (vtransform("object",NN));

    /*Displace*/
    P=P+mag*Km*NN;
    N=calculatenormal(P);
}
```

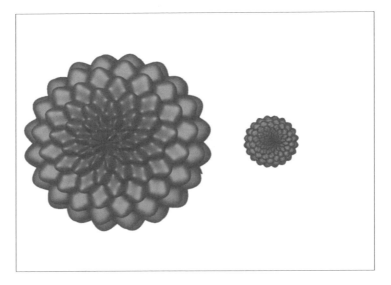

FIGURE 25.5. Displacing in object space

You may find that that when using displacement your objects appear to tear along horizontal and vertical lines. This is caused when the displacement shader moves an object to a part of the image the renderer did not expect it to be in. By the time this is discovered, that part of the image may already have been completed, in which case it is too late to add the displaced object. This can be avoided by warning the renderer about the displacement distance using a RIB command similar to:

```
    Attribute "displacementbound" "sphere" [1]
             "space" ["object"]
```

which specifies that the objects which follow will have points displaced up to a distance of 1 unit in object space.

Not Moving P

As an alternative to actually moving the point, we may choose to simply re-orient the surface at that the point, so that it is lit as if it were displaced, but the points remain in their original position. This approach is called bumping, and while it may not always appear as convincing as true displacement it puts less strain on the rendering engine, and can reduce artifacts. It is also guaranteed to work correctly in surface shaders.

To bump a surface, simply calculate the new surface position, as if for displacement, but do not assign the position back to P. We then use this position, which is typically called PP to calculate the new surface normal. A bumped version of the previous displacement is shown in Listing 25.4. When this is rendered in Figure 25.6 you can see that while bump mapping works well on the smaller object, it becomes obvious that something is wrong, as the sphere becomes larger.

Listing 25.4 A bump shader.

```
displacement simpleBump (
    float Km=0.1;)
{
    vector NN=normalize(N);
    float mag=0;
    point PP;

    /*Calculate mag*/
    mag=sin(s*10*2*PI) * sin(t*10*2*PI);
    mag /= length(vtransform("object",NN));

    /*Displace*/
        PP=P+mag* Km*NN;
    N=calculatenormal(PP);
}
```

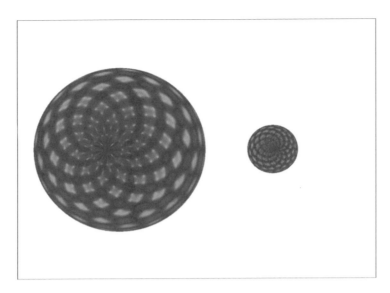

FIGURE 25.6. Bumped spheres

As the processes of bumping and displacing are so similar, it is good practice to provide the user of a displacement shader with the option of either bumping or displacing. You can do this with a simple parameter, as shown in Listing 25.5. This shader incorporates all of the improvements we have made and can be used as a standard template for displacement shaders.

Listing 25.5 A standard displacement shader.

```
displacement standardDisplace (
    float Km=0.1;
    string space="object";
    float trueDisp=1;)
{
    vector NN=normalize(N);
    float mag=0;
    point PP;

    /*Calculate mag*/
        mag=sin(s*10*2*PI)*sin(t*10*2*PI);
    mag /= length(vtransform(space,NN));

    /*Displace*/
    PP=P+mag*Km*NN;
    N=calculatenormal(PP);
    if(trueDisp==1)
        P=PP;
}
```

Summary

```
normal N = calculatenormal(P);
```
Calculates the new surface normal for a surface which has been moved to position P.

```
mag /= length(vtransform("space",normalize(N)));
```
Scale mag so that it's length is now relative to the coordinate system space

```
Attribute "displacementbound" "sphere" [ dist ]
            "space" ["space"]
```
Specifies (in a RIB file) that the following surfaces may be displace up to a distance dist in the coordinate system space.

Chapter 26
Noise

Introduction

The patterns we have developed so far enable us to construct geometric designs on the surface of objects, but even the most carefully manufactured objects have imperfections. It is precisely these imperfections which give real world objects their sense of scale and physical presence. We will now consider how you can use a shader to roughen a surface, avoiding the mathematically perfect appearance that instantly marks an image as computer generated.

Controlled Randomness

To add visual interest to a surface we need to introduce some kind of randomness, but using a standard random function would be of little use. A normal random number would be totally different from frame to frame, and renders would simply not be repeatable. The `cellnoise()` function is works because while it returns an apparently random value, that value is always the same for each cell. This is possible because the cells are based on integers—cell number 1 is always cell 1. However, if we were to attempt to build a similar function which used, for example, the exact value of P to produce a random number, the results would be useless, as P will change minutely from frame to frame.

These problems are solved by a function known as `noise()`. This generates a value which can be used to provide randomness in our textures, but it changes smoothly. Small changes in the input produce small changes in the output, making it tolerant to small movements, and numerical errors.

Noise

The `noise` function in RenderMan can take a varying number of parameters, and return a range of types (much like `cellnoise()`). The values returned are guaranteed to be between 0 and 1, and average 0.5. The value returned is also guaranteed to be 0.5 if the input is a whole number, and will change smoothly between these "lattice points." Within these limitations, the exact values returned by `noise()` are unique to each renderer, but when used correctly, all renderers will produce similar images. A sample from a typical `noise()` function is shown in Figure 26.1.

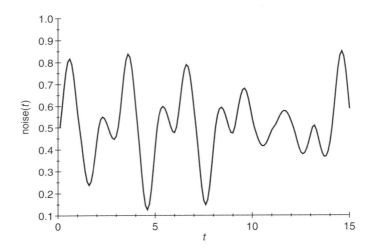

FIGURE 26.1. Noise

You could assign a noise value to `Ct` as in Listing 26.1. This produces a gently changing brightness over the surface. However, by scaling the texture coordinates, as in Figure 26.2 you can produce noise at a range of frequencies. While noise is random at larger scales, it is smooth when viewed more closely. This allows you to use noise to add visual interest at various levels of detail.

Listing 26.1 Noise over a 2D surface.

```
float repeatCount=10;
Ct=float noise(s*repeatCount,t*repeatCount);
```

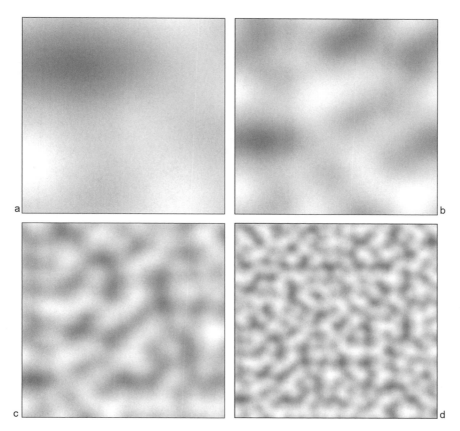

FIGURE 26.2. Noise over a 2D surface at a range of frequencies:
(**a**) repeatCount = 2 (**b**) repeatCount = 4 (**c**) repeatCount = 8 (**d**) repeatCount = 16

In Listing 26.2 we have based the noise value on P rather than s and t, resulting in a noise value which can be used as the basis of a solid texture (Figure 26.3 and Plate VIII). Note how the texture runs smoothly between the two spheres as if they were carved out of a single block of material. We have also used the "`color`" form of `noise()` which returns a color rather than a single floating point value.

Listing 26.2 "Solid"noise.

```
point PP=transform("shader",P);
Ct=color noise(PP*10);
```

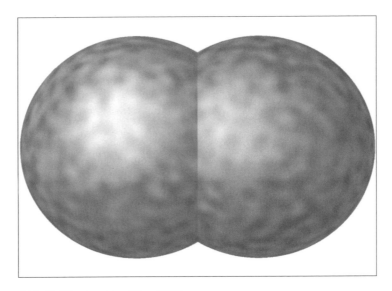

FIGURE 26.3. Solid noise (also Plate VIII)

Distorting Texture Coordinates

Rather than assigning noise directly to a surface, or mixing it into another color, you can also achieve useful results by using noise to distort the texture coordinates. This will break up the straight lines that are generated by simple pattern code. Figure 26.4 (also Plate IX) was created by the shader in Listing 26.3, which uses `noise()` to distort the surface coordinates so that `cellnoise()` produces randomly shaped patches of color, rather than squares. The offset of 100, is added to P in the second `noise()` call, is so that the distortion in t is different to the distortion in s. Any value could be used provided it is reasonably large.

Listing 26.3 Using noise to deform textures.

```
float ss=s+float noise(P*5)*0.5;
float tt=t+float noise(P*5+point(100,100,100))*0.5;
Ct=color cellnoise(ss*10,tt*10);
```

FIGURE 26.4. Using noise to deform textures (also Plate IX)

This approach is incredibly powerful, as it prevents your surfaces from appearing too geometric. For example, it can be used to generate wood textures, by deforming a series of concentric cylinders representing tree rings, as shown in Listing 26.4 and Figure 26.5. As both the noise and cylinders are based upon the value of P rather than surface coordinates, this is a solid texture, giving the appearance that the teapot is made out of wood rather than simply having a wood veneer applied to its surface.

Listing 26.4 A wood texture.

```
color lightWood=color "rgb" (1,0.6,0.5);
color darkWood=color "rgb" (0.3,0.2,0.2);
point PP;
float scale=0.06;
float l;

/*Generate a distored P in shader space*/
PP=transform("shader",P)*scale;
PP=PP+point noise(PP*10)*0.1;

/*Calculate radius*/
l=sqrt(xcomp(PP)*xcomp(PP)+ycomp(PP)*ycomp(PP));

/*mix between light and dark wood*/
Ct=mix(darkWood,lightWood,mod(l*8,1));
```

FIGURE 26.5. A wood texture

Layering Noise

In the real world, surfaces often have many layers of detail, with large-scale course features being further modified by smaller more subtle marks. You can simulate this by applying layers of noise at a range of frequencies as in Figure 26.6. This image was generated by Listing 26.5, which uses a loop to apply six layers of noise at increasingly high frequencies.

Listing 26.5 Layering noise.

```
float i;
float mag=0;
float freq=1;

for(i=0;i<6;i+=1)
    {
    mag+=(float noise(P*freq)-0.5)*2/freq;
    freq*=2.1;
    }
Ct=mag+0.5;
```

FIGURE 26.6. Layering noise

The RenderMan `noise()` function returns a value between 0 and 1 with an average of 0.5, but by subtracting 0.5 and multiplying by two we have scaled it to the range −1 to +1. In most applications of noise other than RenderMan, this is the normal form of noise used. We have used this modified form of noise in Listing 26.5 as its average is 0, so that the average value of `mag` is not changed as more layers are added.

At each layer, the noise value is divided by frequency so that the higher frequency layers have a smaller amplitude than the courser ones. This construct is known as fractional Brownian motion, or more simply fBm, and is used regularly in shaders, as it closely models many structures found in nature. Simply using `mag` as a displacement, as in Listing 26.6, creates a dented appearance as in Figure 26.7.

Listing 26.6 fBm displacement.

```
displacement fbmDisp (
    float Km = 0.1;
    )
{
    vector NN = normalize(N);
    float i;
```

(Continued)

```
float mag=0;
float freq=1;

for(i=0;i<6;i+=1)
    {
    mag+=(float noise(P*freq)-0.5)*2/freq;
    freq*=2.1;
    }

mag /= length(vtransform("object",NN));
P=P+mag*NN*Km
N=calculatenormal(P);
}
```

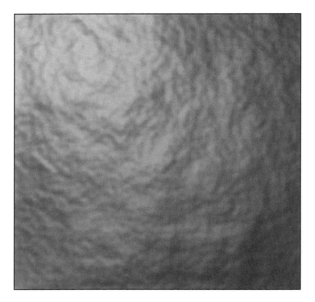

FIGURE 26.7. fBm displacement

Turbulence

A function closely related to fBm is turbulence. This is very similar both in appearance and implementation, but has a more jagged look, as shown in Figure 26.8.

FIGURE 26.8. Turbulence

Examining Listing 26.7 reveals that turbulence is almost exactly the same as fBm but uses the function `abs()` which takes the absolute value, ignoring the sign of the noise. This "folds" the noise creating a discontinuity that makes turbulence appear subtly different to fBm.

Listing 26.7 Turbulence.

```
float i;
float mag=0;
float freq=1;

for(i=0;i<6;i+=1)
    {
    mag+=abs(float noise(P*freq)-0.5)*2/freq;
    freq*=2;
    }
Ct=mag;
```

You can control the exact nature of turbulence and fBm by reducing the number of layers, changing the difference in frequency between layers (known as the lacunarity), or by modifying the value by which each layer is scaled. A generic form of turbulence that incorporates these options as parameters is shown in Listing 26.8.

Listing 26.8 A more flexible turbulence.

```
surface turbulance (
        float layers=4;
        float startingFreq=4;
        float gain=1;
        float lacunarity=1.9132;
            string noiseSpace="shader";
    ...
    )
{
    ...
    float i;
    float mag=0;
    float freq=1;
    point PP=ptransform(noiseSpace,P);
    PP*=startingFreq;

    for(i=0;i<layers;i+=1)
        {
    mag+=abs(float noise(PP*freq)-0.5)*2/pow(freq,gain);
        freq*=lacunarity;
    }
    Ct=mag;
    ...
}
```

One common use of `mag` would be as the blend parameter of a `mix()`. You can also use it to blend between a greater range of colors using the `spline()` function, which takes a variable number of colors (the minimum being four) and uses the first parameter to blend between them, as in Listing 26.9. By selecting the right set of colors this technique can be used to produce a wide range of effects including rock textures such as marble (Figure 26.9 and Plate VII), and flame like textures.

Listing 26.9 Using turbulence with a spline.

```
surface marble (
        float layers=4;
        float startingFreq=1;
        float gain=1;
        float lacunarity=1.9132;
            string noiseSpace="shader";
            float Ka=1;
        float Kd=.5;
        float Ks=.5;
        float roughness=.1;
            color specularcolor=1;
            float scale=0.04)
{
    normal Nf=faceforward (normalize(N),I);
    vector V=-normalize(I);
    color Ct;
    float i;
    float mag=0;
    float freq=startingFreq;
    point PP=ptransform(noiseSpace,P);
    PP*=scale;

    for(i=0;i<layers;i+=1)
        {
            mag+=abs(float noise(PP*freq)-0.5)*2/freq;
        freq*=lacunarity;
    }

    mag=smoothstep(0,0.4,mag);
    Ct=spline(mag,
        color "rgb" (0.25,0.35,0.25),
        color "rgb" (0.25,0.35,0.25),
        color "rgb" (0.20,0.30,0.20),
        color "rgb" (0.20,0.30,0.20),
        color "rgb" (0.20,0.30,0.20),
        color "rgb" (0.25,0.35,0.35),
        color "rgb" (0.25,0.35,0.35),
        color "rgb" (0.15,0.25,0.10),
        color "rgb" (0.15,0.25,0.10),
        color "rgb" (0.10,0.20,0.10),
        color "rgb" (0.10,0.20,0.10),
        color "rgb" (0.25,0.35,0.25),
        color "rgb" (0.10,0.10,0.20)
    );

    Oi=Os;
    Ci=Oi*(Ct*(Ka*ambient()+Kd*diffuse(Nf))
            +specularcolor*
        Ks*specular(Nf,V,roughness));
}
```

FIGURE 26.9. Using turbulance with a spline (also Plate VII)

Summary

```
X=float noise(s);
X=float noise(s,t);
X=float noise(P);
X=float noise(P,t);
```
Generate a pseudo random number based upon either a single parameter, a pair
of texture coordinates, a 3D point, or a point and a number (the number is often
used to represent time, generating a texture which animates from frame to frame).
The value returned will be between 0 and 1, will average 0.5, and will be equal
to 0.5 when all of the parameters are whole numbers.

```
C=color noise(s);
C=color noise(s,t);
C=color noise(P);
C=color noise(P,t);
```
As for `float noise()`, but the value returned is a color.

```
C=spline(t,c1,c2,c3,c4, . . .);
```
Spline blends between a set of colors. The first parameter controls the blend, and
can be followed by any number of colors, with a minimum of 4.

Chapter 27
Aliasing

Introduction

When an object is viewed from far away, in the real world the fine surface detail will become invisible. Unless great care is taken, however, a computer-generated scene will produce unpredictable and ugly results when it contains details that are too small to be fully represented on the screen. This effect, known as "aliasing," is a constant problem for all rendering systems, and has no simple solutions. In this chapter we will look at some techniques you can use in your shaders to try and manage the problem.

What is Aliasing?

We have so far considered shaders as describing a point on the surface, and assumed that the renderer will correctly reconstruct the surface from these points. While this model is adequate for many purposes it falls down when the features we are trying to describe on the surface become so small that they fall between the points that the renderer has picked. Figure 27.1 shows the results of rendering Listing 27.1 (based on on the checkerboard shader we wrote in Chapter 22) at increasingly high values of `repeatCount`. Even at low frequencies the edges of the squares appear ragged, but as the checkerboard pattern becomes finer, the results become very ugly. In certain cases the high frequency pattern can even appear to be of a much lower frequency.

Listing 27.1 A naïve checkerboard shader.

```
float ss=s*repeatCount;
float tt=t*repeatCount;
float sTile=floor(ss);
float tTile=floor(tt);
Ct=mod(sTile+tTile,2);
```

FIGURE 27.1. Aliasing of the checkerboad shader: repeatCount = (**a**) 20 (**b**) 40 (**c**) 80 (**d**) 160 (**e**) 320 (**f**) 640

These artifacts become an even greater problem if you attempt to use the shader in an animation, as they will jump and flicker from frame to frame. Increasing `PixelSamples`, and reducing `ShadingRate` in the RIB file can help by instructing the renderer to use more points, but ultimately, no matter how close together the sampled points are, some features may fall between them.

Rather than considering the shader as describing a collection of points, it is necessary to consider the process of shading as operating on a grid of small squares. In most rendering systems these are known as micropolygons. When the color of the surface is changing slowly then a point sample is a good approximation to the average color of the micropolygon, but if there is too much fine detail (perhaps simply because the camera has moved away from the object) then the approximation will be poor, and the resulting image will suffer from sampling artifacts. Rather than calculating the surface color at a single point the shader should be written to calculate the average color of the square.

Softening Edges

One of the most common ways in which fine detail can be inadvertently introduced into an image is simply by having a sharp edge. If the shader is written to calculate its result at only a single point, it will fail to represent any square which spans the sharp edge correctly. A square which should be 50% in and 50% out of a region will be shaded as completely in or out depending on where the sampling point falls. We have already come across this problem and addressed it by replacing "if" statements with the `smoothstep()` function.

`Smoothstep()` does not calculate the exact proportion of the square that falls on either side of the transition. Instead, it replaces the sharp transition with a more gentle transition such that the point samples can change slowly from being inside to being outside. A point in the middle of the transition will correctly return 0.5, as if it were a square partially overlapping the two regions.

Earlier we used a variable "fuzz" to define the width of the transition region. A large value of fuzz should avoid aliasing but will produce a soft transition resulting in a blurring of the surface detail. The alternative of using a small value of fuzz avoids this blurring but may reintroduce aliasing. While it is perfectly reasonable to hand tune fuzz for a few frames, if the shader needs to operate correctly at a range of resolutions, we need to find an automatic mechanism for generating an appropriate value for fuzz which balances these two extremes.

The information we need to calculate fuzz is provided by the surface coordinates u and v. These are very similar to s and t but are locked to the surface rather than being user defined. The position of the current point sample is determined by u, v while the distance between the point samples is stored in the variables du and dv. For example, if u=0.5 and du=0.1 then the next sample point will have u=0.6. The shader therefore needs to consider a square from u, v to u + du, v + dv, as illustrated in Figure 27.2.

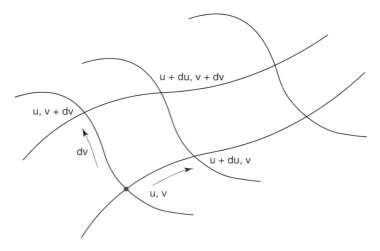

FIGURE 27.2. *u*, *v* and d*u*, d*v*

Though we now know the area we need to consider in terms of u and v, our texture is probably written in terms of ss and tt. The way that any variable changes across the surface can be found using the functions Du() and Dv(). The value returned by Du(ss) approximates how quickly ss is changing in the u-direction—technically known as the partial derivative. The difference between ss at the current point and ss at the next point can therefore be approximated using Du(ss)*du. Ss might also be changing in the v direction, so we arrive at an approximation for "fuzz" (which we will now call filterWidth) by adding together the magnitude of the changes in the two directions.

The code to do this is used in Listing 27.2. Here we have used filterWidth in a shader that uses a sharp step in the top part of the object, and a smoothstep() in the lower part, to make the difference clear. Calculating filterWidth like this produces a near optimal value of fuzz for the smoothstep. We therefore get a transition that is both sharp and alias free (Figure 27.3, also Plate IX). If the object were to be re-rendered at a higher resolution,or you moved the object to be a different size on the screen then filterWidth should automatically adapt.

Listing 27.2 Automatically calculating fuzz.

```
float onRight;

float ss=s+0.1*t;
float filterWidth=abs(Du(ss)*du)+abs(Dv(ss)*dv);
```

```
     if(t>0.5)
        {
        /*Use an IF in the top half to produce a sharp
edge*/
        if(ss>0.5)
            Ct=color "rgb" (0,1,0);
        else
            Ct=Cs;
        }
     else
        {
        /*Use a correctly filtered smooth-step*/
        onRight=smoothstep(0.5-filterWidth,
            0.5+filterWidth,ss);
        Ct=mix(Cs,color "rgb" (0,1,0),onRight);
        }
```

FIGURE 27.3. Automatically calculating fuzz (also Plate IX)

Analytical Antialiasing

As we now know the start and end of the region we are shading and we know the function in between, we should be able to work out the average value over that area. Point sampling provides the most basic approximation.

Consider the simple cosine function shown in Figure 27.4. Provided that we sample it at least twice in each cycle then the approximation of point sampling is reasonably accurate. However, if the frequency of the wave increases then the point samples become a poor fit to the actual signal. To remain accurate we would need to take the point samples closer together. The more samples we take, the better fit we obtain.

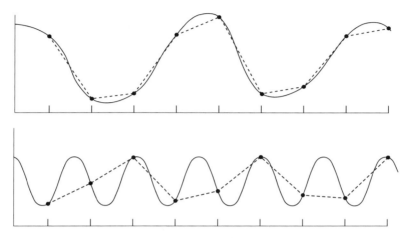

FIGURE 27.4. Sampling Cos(ss)

Theoretically, if we could take an infinite number of samples, then the results would be accurate no matter how the input signal changed. This is exactly what the mathematical technique "integration" does. If we know the original function, and can "integrate" it across the area of the micropolygon then we can accurately average the function. Unfortunately integration is always complex (and often impossible), but we can consider a few simple examples.

To correctly antialias the cos function, we need to evaluate

$$\int_{ss}^{ss + fw} \cos(x)\,dx$$

The integral of cosine is sine and hence the definite integral over this region is:

$$[\sin(x)]_{x = ss}^{ss + fw} = \sin(ss + fw) - \sin(ss)$$

You should then divide this by the width to find the average value over this region:

$$val = \frac{\sin(ss + fw) - \sin(ss)}{fw}$$

Shader code to implement this is shown in Listing 27.3. When ss changes slowly the integrated version of the shader will appear exactly the same as cos(ss), but at higher frequencies the samples of cos(ss) will become effectively random (or worse), while the integrated version will fade to a single uniform color, as shown in Figure 27.5.

Listing 27.3 Point sampling versus antialiasing.

```
float ss=s*scale;
float filterWidth=abs(Du(ss)*du)+abs(Dv(ss)*dv);
float val;
if(s>0.5)
    {
        val=cos(ss);
    }
else
    {
        val=(sin(ss+filterWidth)-sin(ss))
            /filterWidth;
    }
Ct=val*0.5+0.5;
```

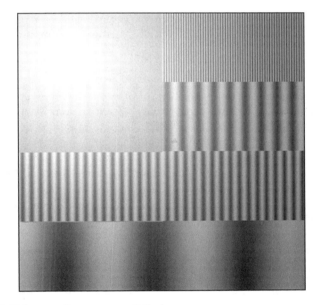

FIGURE 27.5. Point sampling versus antialiasing

   The left-hand side of the image in Figure 27.5 shows four regions of increasing frequency which have been correctly antialiased. The low frequency at the bottom is clearly visible while at the top-left the detailing is so fine that it has correctly blurred out to uniform color. The right-hand side of the image simply uses point sampling, and as the frequency increases the results become inaccurate, eventually producing a completely erroneous image.

Integrating 2D Functions

So far we have considered a function of only one variable, but more often we have a function that varies in both `s` and `t`. When we apply integration to a function of more than one variable, the maths becomes slightly more complex and obscure, as we need to use "vector calculus." Typically, to integrate over a 2D area we have to solve a double integral. For example, in the case of the function `sin(ss)*sin(tt)` we need to evaluate:

$$\int_{ss}^{ss + sFw} \int_{tt}^{tt + tFw} \sin(x) \sin(y) \, dy \, dx$$

This is handled first by integrating with respect to y while considering x to be a constant, giving:

$$\int_{ss}^{ss + sFw} \sin(x) \left[-\cos(y) \right]_{y = tt}^{tt + tFw} dx$$

and then integrating again, this time with respect to x while y remains constant. If we solve this, and divide by the area of the micropolygon we arrive at:

$$val = \frac{(\cos(ss) - \cos(ss + sFw))(\cos(tt) - \cos(tt + tFw))}{sFw.tFw}$$

which is the average value of the function over the micropolygon. While this looks complex, once you have gone through this procedure for a real case you will discover that the cases we have tacked here are in fact particularly simple, and it is generally even more difficult.

The real problem is that while you might think that once you have integrated each function in your shader your aliasing problems are solved, this simply is not the case. While a solution may be available for most individual functions, when several functions are used together (known as composition), you can not simply combine the integrals! More formally, if

$$A(x) = \int a(x) \, dx$$

and

$$B(x) = \int b(x) \, dx$$

then, in the general case

$$A(B(x)) \neq \int a(b(x)) \, dx$$

We should really be integrating the entire shader at once, including the lighting models (a particular source of aliasing for displacement shaders) as a single function. Fortunately all is not lost—we are only interested in the appearance of our objects after all, and in many cases integrating one or more "troublesome" functions within your shader can produce dramatic improvements.

Frequency Clamping

Even for experienced shader writers with a strong mathematical background, analytically antialiasing can be very difficult, or even impossible in many cases. However, many functions have an average value that can be used when viewed from a great distance. When examined at closer range point sampling is adequate. We can therefore simply blend between these two values at the point where the function starts to alias.

If we consider `noise()` it has a feature size of about 1—that is, to get a reasonable approximation to the `noise()` function the filter width would need to be less than approximately 0.5. We can use this knowledge to produce a noise texture that should not alias, as in Listing 27.4. When the filter width is less than 0.2 we have many samples, so the normal value of noise is perfectly adequate. If the filter width is greater than 0.6 then the average value of 0.5 is used. Between these two ranges the noise is faded out gradually.

Listing 27.4 Frequency clamped noise.

```
float filterWidth=abs(Du(ss)*du)+abs(Dv(ss)*dv);
float val;
fade=smoothstep(0.2,0.6,filterWidth);
val=(1-fade)*(float noise(ss))+fade*0.5;
```

This approach is commonly used with fBm, as shown in Listing 27.5. Here we have calculated the noise function based on both `ss` and `tt`, so we need to calculate a filter width in both directions, and fade out the noise based on the largest filter. Rather than recalculating filter width each time round the loop, we simply increase the filter width by `freq`, generating the same result.

Listing 27.5 Frequency clamped fBm.

```
float i;
float freq=1;
float mag=0;
float filterWidthSS=abs(Du(ss)*du)+abs(Dv(ss)*dv);
float filterWidthTT=abs(Du(tt)*du)+abs(Dv(tt)*dv);
float filterWidth=filterWidthSS>filterWidthTT?
                  filterWidthSS:filterWidthTT;
```

(Continued)

```
for(i=0;i<6;i+=1)
    {
    if(s>0.5)
        {
        val=noise(ss*freq,tt*freq);
        }
    else
        {
        fade=smoothstep(0.2,0.6,filterWidth*freq);
        val=(1-fade)*(float noise(ss*freq,tt*freq))
            +fade*0.5;
        }
    mag+=(val-0.5)/freq;
    freq *=2;
    }
Ct=mag+0.5;
```

Examining the results of this shader on the left-hand side of Figure 27.6 you can see that even at low frequencies the antialiased version is a little softer than the point sampled implementation on the right, while at high frequencies the point sampled version is simply random noise.

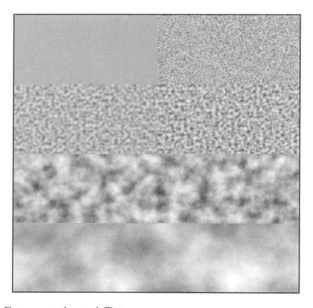

FIGURE 27.6. Frequency clamped fBm

Checkerboard

While the principles of antialiasing are relatively straightforward, actually applying them in practice is somewhat more difficult. We will therefore attempt to
create a checkerboard, similar to the one we have previously constructed, but
avoiding the aliasing problems from which that suffers.

To antialias the checkerboard, we need to consider two aspects—first, we need
to soften the edges of the squares, by using `smoothstep()`. Second, we need
to consider the case where the squares are too small to be adequately represented,
and hence we will use frequency clamping to fade the board to a mid-gray.

If we decide that each square is one unit wide in `ss` and one unit high in `tt`,
then we need to consider the range 0–2 to generate a complete cycle. We will
therefore use `mod()` to create a 2 by 2 tile. Considering one direction at a time,
the obvious thing to do would be to transition from black to white at one and back
to black again at two. This places the transitions at the edges of our 2 by 2 tile,
which may be inconvenient. Instead, at approximately 0.5, we transition from
black to white and at 1.5 we transition from white to back. This can be done using
the code in Listing 27.6, which generates a set of vertical stripes as in Figure 27.7.
By duplication of this code in `tt` we could generate horizontal stripes.

Listing 27.6 Vertical stripes.

```
float  repeatCount = 40;
float  ss = s*repeatCount + t;
float  filterWidthSS = abs(Du(ss)*du) + abs(Dv(ss)*dv);
float  smag;

ss = mod(ss,2);
smag = smoothstep(0.5 - filterWidthSS,
                  0.5 + filterWidthSS,ss);
smag -= smoothstep(1.5 - filterWidthSS,
                  1.5 + filterWidthSS,ss);

Ct = smag;
```

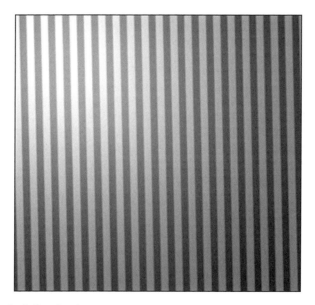

FIGURE 27.7. Antialiased stripes

In Listing 27.7 we combine these horizontal and vertical stripes into squares. To do this we need to scale `smag` and `tmag` into the range −1 to +1, multiply them together, and then scale back into the standard 0–1 range. By doing this we get a check pattern, as in Figure 27.8. This works because when `smag` and `tmag` are the same we get a white square, while if they are different we get a black square—an operation known as an Exclusive OR (Figure 27.9).

Listing 27.7 A basic checkerboard.

```
float  repeatCount=40;
float  ss=s*repeatCount+t;
float  tt=t*repeatCount-s;
float  filterWidthSS=abs(Du(ss)*du)+abs(Dv(ss)*dv);
float  filterWidthTT=abs(Du(tt)'du)+abs(Dv(tt)*dv);
float  smag,tmag;

ss=mod(ss,2);
tt=mod(tt,2);

smag=smoothstep(0.5-filterWidthSS,0.5+
filterWidthSS,ss);
smag-=smoothstep(1.5-filterWidthSS,1.5+
filterWidthSS,ss);
smag=smag*2-1;

tmag=smoothstep(0.5-filterWidthTT,0.5+
filterWidthTT,tt);
tmag-=smoothstep(1.5-filterWidthTT,1.5+
filterWidthTT,tt);
tmag=tmag*2-1;

Ct=(smag*tmag)/2+0.5;
```

FIGURE 27.8. A basic checkerboard

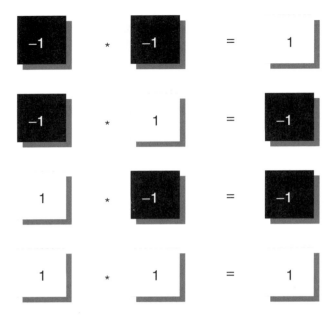

FIGURE 27.9. An Exclusive OR function

We now need to consider how the pattern will fade out as filter width increases. Earlier we used the worst case filter width from the ss and tt directions, but here we can filter each separately. This is a better approach as, due to the orientation of the surface or the choice of different scales in the s and t directions, the filter widths might not be the same.

One complete cycle of the stripes has a width of two and hence we must have a filter width of less than one to accurately reproduce them. We therefore fade smag and tmag to their mid-value as filterwidth reaches one. The resultant shader is shown in Listing 27.8 is a significant improvement on the version in Listing 27.1, as can be seen by comparing Figure 27.1 to the results in Figure 27.10.

Listing 27.8 The completed checkerboard.

```
surface check (
    float repeatCount = 40;

    float Ka = 1;
    float Kd = .5;
    float Ks = .5;
    float roughness = .1;
    color specularcolor = 1;)
{
    normal Nf = faceforward (normalize(N),I);
    vector V = -normalize(I);
    color Ct;

    float ss=s*repeatCount+t;
    float tt=t*repeatCount-s;
    float filterWidthSS=abs(Du(ss)*du)+abs(Dv(ss)*dv);
    float filterWidthTT=abs(Du(tt)*du)+abs(Dv(tt)*dv);
    float smag,tmag;

    ss=mod(ss,2);
    tt=mod(tt,2);
    smag=smoothstep(0.5-filterWidthSS,0.5+
    filterWidthSS,ss);
    smag-=smoothstep(1.5-filterWidthSS,1.5+
    filterWidthSS,ss);
    smag=smag*2-1;
    smag*=1-smoothstep(0.4,1.2,filterWidthSS);

    tmag = smoothstep(0.5-filterWidthTT,0.5 +
    filterWidthTT,tt);
    tmag -= smoothstep(1.5 - filterWidthTT,1.5 +
    filterWidthTT,tt);
    tmag = tmag*2-1;
    tmag*=1-smoothstep(0.4,1.2,filterWidthTT);

    Ct=(smag*tmag)/2+0.5;

    Oi = Os;
    Ci = Oi * ( Ct * (Ka*ambient() + Kd*diffuse(Nf)) +
        specularcolor * Ks*specular(Nf,V,roughness));
}
```

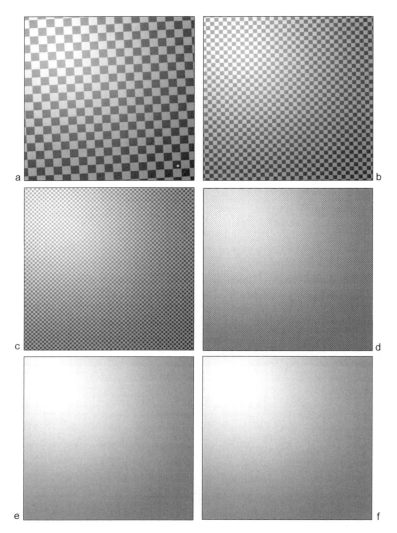

FIGURE 27.10. An antialiased checkerboad shader: repeat Count = (**a**) 20 (**b**) 40 (**c**) 80
(**d**) 160 (**e**) 320 (**f**) 640

Summary

Anti-aliasing is an on-going problem to which there are no simple answers. In
every shader a trade off must be made between the quality of the final image, the
range of shots for which the shader will be viable, the shader development time,
and the render time.

Chapter 28
Shading Models

Introduction

In many cases the standard plastic-like shading model will suffice, at least during initial shader development. As you progress, however, you shall want to refine the way light interacts with your surface. RenderMan allows you to interrogate each of the lights in the scene, and hence shade your surface in any way you feel is appropriate.

Inside the Standard Models

The `diffuse()` and `specular()` functions typically used to calculate the shading of a surface collect the light from each of the light sources within the scene and for each one work out how much will be reflected towards the camera. While having this process automated for us is very convenient, if you need to create new lighting models—for example, an anisotropic surface which reflects light only in certain directions—then it is necessary to break open these functions and implement them explicitly.

Diffuse

The standard diffuse model is defined such that the contribution from each light is:

```
Cl*normalize(L).normalize(N)
```

That is, the color of the light multiplied by the dot product of the incident light vector and the surface normal. To turn this into useful code we need to put this inside a loop that visits each light in turn. This is done in Listing 28.1. `Illuminance` is a looping construct unique to SL, which loops over all of the lights in the scene that are visible from the point being shaded.

Listing 28.1 Diffuse `Illuminance` model.

```
color Cdiff=0;
illuminance(P,Nf,PI/2)
    {
         Cdiff+=Cl*normalize(L).Nf;
    }
```

The three parameters to `Illuminance` are the point being shaded, the direction of interest and an angle. These three variables define a cone, as shown in Figure 28.1. Any lights outside this cone are excluded from the loop. Within the loop, the new global variables `Cl` and `L` are setup representing the color of the light, and a vector from the surface to the light source. We simply need to apply the lighting model of our choice and add that to the total light recorded so far.

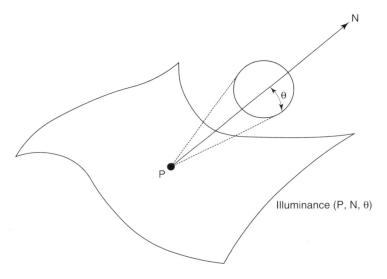

FIGURE 28.1. The parameters to `illuminance`

Specular

Similarly, we can build our own specular function as shown in Listing 28.2. This uses vector `H`, which is half way between the observer vector `V` and the direction to the light `L`. This vector `H` represents the orientation that the surface normal would need to be to produce the optimal reflection. We can find how far away the actual surface normal is from this ideal value by taking the dot product of `H` and `N` to produce a value that gets smaller as we move away from the mirror angle. This value is then raised to a power to control the size of the specular highlight.

Listing 28.2 Specular `Illuminance` model.

```
color Cspec=0;

illuminance(P,Nf,PI/2)
{
vector H=normalize(V+normalize(L));
Cspec+=Cl*pow(H. Nf,1/roughness);
}
```

This lighting model is equivalent to the official RenderMan specular function, but may not correspond to the highlights produced by a particular renderer, as many use slightly different code to produce highlights which are subjectively more pleasing.

Custom Illumination Models

Since the orientation for the surface and the direction of each incident light is known, you can combine these together in any way you see fit to produce the lighting model of your choice. You could start with a physical model of how light interacts with a surface and try and implement it, or simply tweak one of the existing models to produce something that looks good.

One interesting group of illumination models are known as anisotropic. Whereas most surfaces reflect light equally in all orientations, some, such as a vinyl record or compact disc reflect light in a highly directional way. This is usually due to some fine detail such as the record's grooves which would be too small to actually render directly but have a major effect on the surface's appearance.

To create such a surface we need to factor the orientation of the surface coordinates into the lighting model. For example, consider a surface made from highly reflective threads like satin. To recreate such a surface you would need to consider how the incident light is oriented to these threads rather than to the surface normal.

If we assume that the threads run in the u direction then we can find the direction of the threads in 3D space using `Du(P)`. If we normalize `Du(P)` and take the dot product with `H` (as in the standard specular function) we would get a lighting model which was brightest when the light was shining along the threads. In fact, we want to maximize the highlight when the `H` is at 90° to the thread, and hence we use a scale factor of:

```
sqrt(1-pow(H.dir,2))
```

This lighting model is used as part of the shader in Listing 28.3, which also includes ambient and diffuse components. Note how the highlights are stretched along the surface when this is applied to the teapot model in Figure 28.2. Figure 28.3 (also Plate X) shows the result of applying an identical shader, but with the threads oriented in the v direction by setting `dir=normalize(Dv(P))`

Listing 28.3 An anisotropic surface.

```
surface satinU (
    float roughness = 0.1;
    color specularcolor = 1;)
{
    normal Nf = faceforward (normalize(N),I);
    vector V = -normalize(I);
    color Caniso = 0;
    vector dir=normalize(Du(P));

    illuminance(P,Nf,PI/2)
        {
        vector H=normalize(V+normalize(L));
        float scale=sqrt(1-(H.dir*H.dir));
        Caniso+=Cl*pow(scale,1/roughness);
        }

    Oi = Os;
    Ci = Os * (Caniso+Cs*(ambient()+0.2*diffuse(Nf)));
}
```

FIGURE 28.2. An anisotropic surface

FIGURE 28.3. Reorienting the satin shader (also Plate X)

Summary

```
illuminance(P,dir,theta) { . . . }
```
An `illiminance` loop, iterates over all light sources visible from the point P, within `theta` radians of the direction `dir`.

```
Cl
```
Within an illuminance loop `Cl` contains the color of the incident light from the current source.

```
L
```
Within an illuminance loop `L` points to the light source from the surface point being shaded.

Chapter 29
Other Kinds of Shader

Introduction

So far we have concentrated on surface shaders as these are by far the most common. However, RenderMan also allows shaders to control other parts of the rendering process. In this chapter you will see how light shaders can be used to define the behavior of light sources, while a volume shader can modify the observed color of a surface due to atmospheric effects such as fog.

Volume Shaders

The images we see are not always the simple result of light bouncing from hard surfaces. Often the light is modified in some way as it passes through the air, perhaps by smoke or fog. To describe the properties of the space through which light travels, RenderMan provides volume shaders.

The most common use of a volume shader is to describe the effect of the space between a surface and the camera by modifying the color of a surface after it has been calculated by the surface shader. A volume shader therefore does its work by modifying Ci. When used in this way it is known as an "atmosphere".

For maximum flexibility atmosphere shaders are applied on a per object basis using the Attribute command:

```
Atmosphere "myDepthShader"
```

In principle this means you can can attach different fogging effects to each object, but unless you are attempting something unusual it is probably best to apply one atmosphere shader to the whole scene. You should also be aware that if there is no object covering a particular part of the image, then it will not be fogged, as there is nothing there to attach the shader to. To avoid this strange effect, it is common to place a large sphere around the whole scene when atmosphere shaders are being used.

One of the simplest descriptions of an atmosphere would be to fade out objects beyond a certain point. We can do this by considering the length of I—the vector from the camera to the shaded point. If this is less than a certain distance then Ci should remain unchanged, beyond a second distance you should replace it with the background color. In the mid-region, we blend the two together using mix() and smoothstep(), as shown in Listing 29.1 and Figure 29.1 (also Plate IX). As always, when dealing with vectors we should specify a coordinate space to ensure consistency between renderers.

Listing 29.1 A simple depth fade shader.

```
volume
depthfade (float mindistance = 1;
           float maxdistance = 9;
           color background = color "rgb" (1,1,1);)
{
    float d;
    vector Icam = vtransform("camera",I);
    d = smoothstep(mindistance, maxdistance,
                   length(Icam));
    Ci = mix (Ci, background, d);
    Oi = mix (Oi, color(1,1,1), d);
}
```

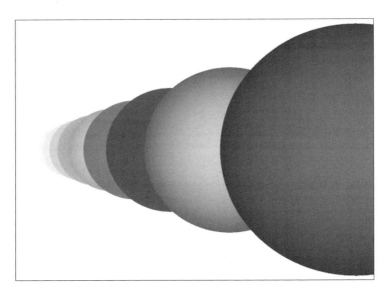

FIGURE 29.1. A simple depth fade (also Plate IX)

A slightly more realistic effect would be to consider that as an object moves away through a foggy atmosphere, it becomes increasingly faint, but never disappears completely. This exponential effect is produced by the "fog" shader shown in Figure 29.2 (also Plate IX) and Listing 29.2.

Listing 29.2 A fog shader.

```
volume fog (float distance = 1;
            color background = 0;)
  {
  vector Icam=vtransform("camera",I);
  float d = 1 - exp (-length(Icam)/distance);
  Ci = mix (Ci, background, d);
  Oi = mix (Oi, color(1,1,1), d);
  }
```

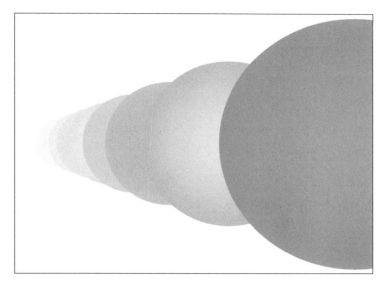

FIGURE 29.2. A fog effect (also Plate IX)

Though these shaders are very simple, volume shaders can use all of the techniques available to regular shaders. You could, for example, examine the position of the point being shaded, and use that to define a layer of fog, rather than fogging the whole scene equally.

Light Shaders

In addition to controlling the appearance of surfaces, you can also use shaders to control the light sources in your scene. While a surface shader's job is to calculate the observed color of a surface, a light shader's job is to decide how much light a particular source casts upon a point.

Pointlights

The simplest interesting light shader is the `pointlight`. The code for this is shown in Listing 29.3. A `pointlight` is defined by a position, an intensity and a color, which are provided by parameters. From these the shader must calculate a value for `Cl` and `L` which will be passed to the surface shader for use in an `illuminance` loop, or one of the standard lighting functions.

Listing 29.3 A pointlight source.

```
light pointlight (
    float intensity = 1;
    color lightcolor = 1;
    point from = point "shader" (0,0,0);)
{
    illuminate (from)
        {
        Cl = intensity * lightcolor/(L.L);
        }
}
```

In most cases light shaders make use of an `illuminate` statement. This looks a lot like the `illuminance` loop we used to collect light in a surface shader. In the case of the pointlight, we tell `illuminate` the position of our light source. This automatically sets up `L` to be the vector from the light source's position to the surface. From this, we calculate the color of the light hitting the surface by multiplying the light's intensity by its color. We divide by `L.L`, as this provides a natural fall-off in light intensity as can be seen in Figure 29.3 (also Plate IX).

FIGURE 29.3. A point light (also Plate IX)

Although the standard `pointlight` shader exhibits a physically accurate illumination pattern, there is no reason why this need be the case. In fact nonphysically realistic lights can be far easier to work with. As an example of this in Listing 29.4 we have created a light that only casts light on surfaces which are between two and three units away. In addition it does not fall away as quickly. You could use such a shader to light an area in a more even fashion than the standard pointlight, as it avoids the extremes of light and dark. However, as can be seen in Figure 29.4 (also Plate IX), the lack of physical realism can make the scene appear strange.

Listing 29.4 A nonphysical light.

```
light nearfarlight (
    float intensity = 1;
    color lightcolor = 1;
    float near = 2;
    float far = 3;
    point from = point "shader" (0,0,0);)
{
    float length;
    float brightness;

    illuminate (from)
```

(Continued)

```
    {
        length=sqrt(L.L);
        if(length<near || length>far)
            brightness = 0;
        else
            brightness = 1/length;
    Cl = intensity * lightcolor*brightness;
    }
}
```

FIGURE 29.4. A Nonphysical light (also Plate IX)

Spotlights

A second form of `illuminate` statement allows you to specify not only a position for the light, but also a direction and a cone angle. Only those points within the cone will be illuminated. Not only is this an easy way to create a simple spotlight, it is also efficient, as it allows the renderer to skip the calculations for points which are not going to be lit.

Such an illuminate statement is used in Listing 29.5. Only points within 30° of the light's axis are illuminated, creating the illumination pattern seen in Figure 29.5 (also Plate IX). While this shader does create a beam of light, the edges of that beam are sharp and unattractive. The standard spotlight incorporates additional code to smoothly transition between the area inside the beam and the areas that are not lit.

Listing 29.5 A conical beamlight.

```
light
beamlight ( float intensity = 1;
            color lightcolor = 1;
            point from = point "shader" (0,0,0);
            point to = point "shader" (0,0,1);
            )
{

    uniform vector A = normalize(to-from);

    illuminate (from, A, radians(30))
        {
            Cl = intensity * lightcolor/(L.L);
        }

}
```

FIGURE 29.5. A conical beam (also Plate IX)

Having created some basic light sources, you are free to modify the resultant light in any way you feel appropriate. For example, you could use a texture to project an image into the scene. In Listing 29.6 we have used the angle between the axis and the L vector to modify the light's color, producing the pattern of lighting seen in Figure 29.6 (also Plate IX).

Listing 29.6 Modifying a light's color.

```
light colorlight (
    float intensity = 1;
    point from = point "shader" (0,0,0);
    point to = point "shader" (0,0,1);
    )
{
    float cosangle;
    color lightcolor;
    uniform vector A = normalize(to-from);
    illuminate (from, A, radians(30))
        {
        cosangle = (L.A)/length(L);
        lightcolor = color "hsv" (cosangle*10,1,1);
        Cl = intensity * lightcolor/(L.L) ;
        }
}
```

FIGURE 29.6. Modifying a lights color (also Plate IX)

Shadows

One of the most common modifications is the addition of support for shadow maps. Having created a shadow map as described in Chapter 14, actually using it is remarkably simple. By simply passing the name of a map to the `shadow` function, as in Listing 29.7 you can obtain a value indicating to what extent a point is in shadow. Within a light shader `Ps` represents the point on the surface being lit, and hence `1-shadow("shadowmap",  Ps)` calculates to what extent the point should be illuminated. This value is simply factored into the lighting calculation.

Listing 29.7 Creating a shadow.

```
light shadowlight (
    float intensity = 1;
    color lightcolor = 1;
    point from = point "shader" (0,0,0);
    point to = point "shader" (0,0,1);
    string shadowname = "";
    )
{

    float atten;
    uniform vector A = normalize(to-from);

    illuminate (from, A, radians(30))
        {
        if(shadowname != "")
            atten=1-shadow(shadowname,Ps);
        else
            atten=1;
        Cl = atten*intensity * lightcolor/(L.L) ;
        }
}
```

If the map name "raytrace" is used, then the shadow will be calculated directly by ray tracing, rather than using an actual map file.

Summary

```
illuminate(P) {. . .}
illuminate(P,A,angle) {. . .}
```
Illuminate works out which points should be illuminated, either in all directions from the point P or within angle of an axis A. L is automatically calculated, and Cl must be calculated within the following braces.

```
float shad=shadow("mapname",Ps)
```
Calculates to what degree the point Ps is in shadow. The incident light for the point is usually multiplied by 1-shad.

Related Functions

solar(direction,angle)

Not all lights have a position. The solar statement serves a similar function to illuminate but does not require a position. It is used to create distant lights such as the sun.

Chapter 30
Global Illumination

Introduction

In recent years most RenderMan implementations have added support for global illumination (GI)—that is the calculation of effects produced by light interacting with several surfaces before it reaches the camera. This allows more realistic images to be produced at the cost of additional rendering time.

Because GI is potentially very slow to render, it has been incorporated into the RenderMan standard in such a way that effects can be controlled on per object basis. Only those objects which require GI need use it, while objects which can be accurately rendered with standard techniques continue to be rendered at high speed. In this chapter we will see how you can enable ray-traced shadows, reflections, caustics, and bounce light using the shading language.

Shadows

As we saw in Chapter 14, ray-traced shadows can be implicitly integrated into lights by using "`raytrace`" as the name of a shadow map. When the shadow function is called with this map, the value returned is calculated directly by ray tracing, rather than using a real shadow map file.

Not all objects need be included in the calculation of ray traced shadows. We can improve performance by manually excluding some objects as potential casters of shadows. For example, in Figure 30.1 (also Plate X) the ground plane cannot cast shadows on the teapot or itself, so in Listing 30.1 we have marked it as transparent for the purposes of ray-tracing shadows. Performance is improved, but the resulting image is correctly shadowed. The Attribute group "`visibility`" is used to control which objects are use in different rendering situations. In the case of shadow rays, the "`transmission`" controls whether objects cast shadows. This attribute can take four possible values of progressing complexity:

245

Listing 30.1 Ray-Traced Shadows.

```
Display "shadow.tiff" "file" "rgba"
Projection "perspective" "fov" [ 30 ]

Rotate -20 1 0 0
Translate 0 -1 5
WorldBegin
    LightSource "ambientlight" 1 "intensity" [ 0.1 ]
    LightSource "shadowspot" 2
        "shadowname" [ "raytrace" ]
        "from" [ 2 4 0 ]
        "to" [ 0 0 0 ]
        "intensity" [ 7 ]
        "coneangle" [0.3]
        "conedeltaangle" [0.05]

    Surface "plastic"
    Attribute "visibility" "transmission" [ "opaque" ]
    ReadArchive "teapot.rib"

    Color [ 0 1 0 ]
    Attribute "visibility" "transmission" [ "transparent" ]
    Patch "bilinear" "P" [ -5 -1 -5
                            5 -1 -5
                           -5 -1  5
                            5 -1  5 ]
WorldEnd
```

FIGURE 30.1. Ray-traced shadows (also Plate X)

"transparent"—the object does not cast ray-traced shadows
"opaque"—the object casts shadows, and is considered as fully opaque
"Os"—the object casts shadows but is semitransparent, as defined in the RIB file
"shader"—the object casts shadows and its transparency varies over the surface

In addition to "transparent" and "opaque," for the purposes of ray-traced shadows objects may be semitransparent. When the "Os" transmission value is used then the transparency for shadows is that set by the Opacity command. If "shader" is used then a full surface shading calculation is performed upon this surface to determine its opacity. In addition to using the "raytrace" shadow map you can explicitly test the visibility between two points using the function transmission(Psrc, Pdest). This calculates how much light can be transmitted between Psrc and Pdest.

Mirror Reflections

Perhaps the most obvious use of GI is to produce mirror reflections in highly polished surfaces. To calculate these, you simply need to find the direction of the reflection (using reflect(), as we did for environment maps in Chapter 24), and fire a ray using the trace() function to find the color of the scene in that direction. A simple shader which does this is shown in Listing 30.2.

Listing 30.2 A Reflective Shader.

```
surface reflect (
    float Ka = 1;
        float Kd = .2;
        float Ks = .7;
        float Kr = .3;
        float roughness = .1;
    color specularcolor = 1;)
{
    normal Nf = faceforward (normalize(N),I);
    vector V = -normalize(I);
    color Ct;

    vector R = normalize(reflect(I,Nf));
    color Cr = trace(P,R);

    Ct = Cs;
    Oi = Os;
    Ci = Oi * ( Ct * (Ka*ambient() + Kd*diffuse(Nf)) +
        specularcolor * (Ks*specular(Nf,V,roughness) +
        Kr*Cr));
}
```

We have applied this shader in Listing 30.3. Just as with ray-traced shadows it is important to control which objects are included in ray traced reflections. In this case the ground is reflected in the teapot (as seen in Figure 30.2, also Plate X), so the "reflect" shader has been applied to the teapot. However, to keep render times managable, the teapot will not itself be visible in those reflections. This is controlled with the "visibility"/"trace" Attribute. To make the teapot invisible in reflections we have used:

```
Attribute "visibility" "trace" [ 0 ]
```

While the gound plane has the Attribute

```
Attribute "visibility" "trace" [ 1 ]
```

It is also possible to implicity ray trace reflections by using a mapname of "raytrace" with the environment() function.

Listing 30.3 Ray traced reflections.

```
Display "raytrace.tiff" "file" "rgba"
Projection "perspective" "fov" [ 30 ]

Rotate -20 1 0 0
Translate 0 -1 5
WorldBegin
    LightSource "ambientlight" 1 "intensity" [ 0.1 ]
    LightSource "shadowspot" 2
        "shadowname" [ "raytrace" ]
            "from" [ 2 4 0 ]
            "to" [ 0 0 0 ]
            "intensity" [ 7 ]
            "coneangle" [0.3]
            "conedeltaangle" [0.05]

    Surface "reflect"
    Attribute "visibility" "trace" [ 0 ]
    Attribute "visibility" "transmission" [ "opaque" ]
    ReadArchive "teapot.rib"

    Surface "plastic"
    Color [ 0 1 0 ]
    Attribute "visibility" "trace" [ 1 ]
    Attribute "visibility" "transmission" [ "transparent" ]
    Patch "bilinear" "P" [ -5 -1 -5
                            5 -1 -5
                           -5 -1  5
                            5 -1  5 ]

WorldEnd
```

FIGURE 30.2. Ray-traced reflections (also Plate X)

Soft Reflections

The trace() function probes the scene in a single direction, which produces a mirror like reflection. However, in the real world surfaces are rarely so highly polished. A slightly rougher surface would reflect light in a range of directions. We can simulate this by tracing several rays in slightly different directions, and combining them to produce a slightly blurred reflection.

While its possible to do this in SL using trace(), it is slightly more tricky to implement correctly than it would at first appear. To make things easier (and more efficient) the "gather" statement has been added to the RenderMan API. This fires a number of rays distributed over a cone and allows you to combine the results in a flexable fashion. Listing 30.4 calculates a reflection color (Cr) using gather, and while it is more complex than trace(), it is also significantly more powerful. A number of rays (in this case 15) are traced from the point P in the direction R, plus or minus the cone angle (10°). For each ray that is traced that hits an object, a surface shader is run, and the resulting color is copied from Ci *in that shader* to Chit in this one. Of course, you are not just restricted to interrogating Ci—you can obtain virtually any parameter of the hit surface.

Listing 30.4 The gather statement.

```
color Cr=0;
color Chit;
float samples=15;
vector R=normalize(reflect(I,Nf));
float hits=0;
gather("illuminance", P, R, radians(10), samples,
        "surface:Ci", Chit)
    {
    Cr+=Chit;
    hits+=1;
    }
else
        {
Cr+=color "rgb" (0.5,0.5,0.5);
        hits+=1;
        }
Cr=Cr/hits;
```

Rather than just returning a single value like trace, gather allows you to process the results of each hit. The code block following gather is executed each time a ray hits a surface, and while we have chosen to simply add up the colors found for each hit, you can use any code you like here. This block is equivalent to an illuminance loop, and you could use it to implement similar local illumination models.

Of course not all rays hit objects. In our test scene, rays which are reflected upwards miss the ground plane, and there is no surface color to calculate. This is the main reason Figure 30.2 looks slightly strange—the empty space of the sky is white, but the top of the teapot does not reflect it. The gather statement takes care of this with an else clause. If the ray does not hit any object at all, then the second block of code is executed, which in this case adds a constant background color. You could use an environment map here. This would allows you to ray trace between important foreground objects, but fall back to a much simpler environment map for distant parts of your scene which are less significant.

In Figure 30.3 (also Plate X) the top of the teapot is lighter as a result of the "misses" being correctly handled, and the edges of the reflected shadows are softer.

FIGURE 30.3. Tracing multiple rays (also Plate X)

When using ray-traced reflections it is important to watch out of the explosion of rays: one ray from the camera creates 10 reflected rays which each create 10 further rays. Suddenly over 100 rays need to be traced and 100 surfaces shaded, and the scene becomes unrenderable in the available time. This must be managed carefully, only ray tracing essential objects. Additionally, you can use the `raylevel()` function in your shaders to test if you are rendering a camera ray, a first generation reflection or some deeper, more complex inter-reflection. As the value returned by `raylevel()` increases you should simplify your shader, and consider removing ray tracing all together. For example you could add:

```
float samples=10/(raylevel()+1);
```

to Listing 30.4, so that less rays are fired for as the depth of reflection increases.

As a safety control to ensure that ray tracing actually completes, and does not spend hours bouncing light between two parallel surfaces, there are limits on how many levels of reflection will be calculated. The global limit is set in the RIB file by:

```
Option "trace" "maxdepth" [ 10 ]
```

It can further be reduced on a per object using

```
Attribute "trace" "maxspeculardepth" [ 2 ]
```

It is also possible to use simplified geometry during ray tracing. Simply make the complex object invisible to traced rays, then add a simpler object which is made invisible to the camera using the Attribute

```
Attribute "visibility" "camera" [ 0 ]
```

Bounce Light

While in theory it would be possible to use ray tracing to calculate all of the lighting effects within a scene it becomes particular inefficient when diffuse surfaces are used. These scatter light in a wide range of directions requiring far too many rays to be traced. Rather than writing shaders which trace rays looking for light it would be far more efficient to start with the light sources (where we *know* there is lots of light), and see where the light goes. This is achieved using photon maps. Like shadow maps, photon maps are precalculated in a separate render pass which records where light bounces from diffuse surfaces. These maps are then interrogated by shaders in the final beauty pass. Listing 30.5 shows our scene modified to generate a photon map.

Listing 30.5 Generating a photon map.

```
Hider "photon" "emit" [ 1000000 ]
Display "photon.tiff" "file" "rgba"
Projection "perspective" "fov" [ 30 ]

Attribute "photon" "globalmap" ["photon.gpm"]
Rotate -20 1 0 0
Translate 0 -1 5
WorldBegin
    LightSource "ambientlight" 1 "intensity" [ 0.1 ]
    LightSource "shadowspot" 2
        "shadowname" [ "raytrace" ]
            "from" [ 2 4 0 ]
            "to" [ 0 0 0 ]
            "intensity" [ 7 ]
            "coneangle" [0.3]
            "conedeltaangle" [0.05]

    Surface "reflect"
    Attribute "visibility" "photon" [ 1 ]
    Attribute "photon" "shadingmodel" "matte"
    Attribute "visibility" "trace" [ 0 ]
    Attribute "visibility" "transmission" [ "opaque" ]
    ReadArchive "teapot.rib"

    Surface "plastic"
    Attribute "visibility" "photon" [ 1 ]
    Attribute "photon" "shadingmodel" "matte"
    Color [ 0 1 0 ]
    Attribute "visibility" "trace" [ 1 ]
    Attribute "visibility" "transmission" [ "transparent"
]
    Patch "bilinear" "P" [ -5 -1 -5
                            5 -1 -5
                           -5 -1  5
                            5 -1  5 ]
WorldEnd
```

We have set the `Hider` to be "`photon`," instructing the render to generate a map. 10,00,000 particles are generated, allowed to bounce round the scene to simulate the light, and then stored in the file "`photon.gpm`." As both the teapot and the ground will be used to bounce light around, we have set:

```
Attribute "visibility" "photon" [ 1 ]
```

on both objects.

Though we have used a lot of particles, the photon mapping process is very simple, and relies on huge numbers of photons to do the work. While you should consider if fewer photons can be used for any particular scene, in this case the render times are still short enough that we need not be too concerned. To speed up the photon mapping process full shading is avoided by specifying that simplified shaders built into the renderer are used during photon mapping, rather than user defined SL shaders. In this case, we have specified that the objects both behave as matte objects using the RIB command:

```
Attribute "photon" "shadingmodel" "matte"
```

The simple shading models available will typically include matte, metal, plastic, and glass but this is highly renderer dependant.

Having generated a photon map, to use it in a shader, we simply call the function `photonmap()`, providing the name of the map, the point we are shading and the surface normal, as in Listing 30.6. This returns the light at the surface, as calculated during the map generation pass. As the main light sources have been included in the photon map, we only need to add ambient light to get a fully illuminated scene.

Listing 30.6 Using a photon map.

```
surface photon (float Kd=0.75;
                float Ka=1;
                string mapname="photon.gpm")
    {
    normal Nf=faceforward(normalize(N),I);
    Oi=Os;
    Ci=Cs*(Kd*photonmap(mapname,P,Nf)+Ka*ambient())
        *Oi;
    }
```

If we attach the photon shader to the objects in our scene we get the image in Figure 30.4 (also Plate X). The lighting is much softer than produced by ray tracing, as some of the darker areas have been filled in by bounce light. This is most noticeable on the underside of the teapot lid's handle.

FIGURE 30.4. Bounced light (also Plate X)

Bringing it all Together

Though photon maps can efficiently approximate complex lighting, the results are often noisy, as can be seen by the dappled effect in Figure 30.4. While using more photons can improve this to some degree, a better approach is to combine photon mapping with ray tracing. In parts of the scene where quality is most important, we can fire lots of rays, while in less critical areas (for example, on objects which are themselves visible through reflections), we can use photon maps to produce a quick approximation without generating any more rays.

While you could implement this explicitly in SL, this approach has been bundled up in the `indirectdiffuse()` function. Simply calling this function will trace rays in all directions. However, after a small number of bounces (usually only one), we stop ray tracing to avoid huge render times. Depending on the implementation, a photon map can then be used to complete the calculation. The depth limit is controlled by:

```
Attribute "trace" "maxdiffusedepth" [ 2 ]
```

while the map used to complete the calculation is set with:

```
Attribute "photon" "globalmap" [ "photon.pmap"]
```

as in Listing 30.7.

Listing 30.7 Generating a photon map.

```
Display "indirect.tiff" "file" "rgba"
Projection "perspective" "fov" [ 30 ]

Rotate -20 1 0 0
Translate 0 -1 5
WorldBegin
    LightSource "ambientlight" 1 "intensity" [ 0.1 ]
    LightSource "shadowspot" 2
        "shadowname" [ "raytrace" ]
            "from" [ 2 4 0 ]
            "to" [ 0 0 0 ]
            "intensity" [ 7 ]
            "coneangle" [0.3]
            "conedeltaangle" [0.05]

    Attribute "trace" "maxdiffusedepth" [ 2 ]
    Attribute "photon" "globalmap" [ "photon.gpm"]
    Surface "indirect"
    Attribute "visibility" "trace" [ 0 ]
    Attribute "visibility" "photon" [ 1 ]
    Attribute "visibility" "transmission" [ "opaque" ]
    ReadArchive "teapot.rib"

    Surface "indirect"
    Color [ 0 1 0 ]
    Attribute "visibility" "trace" [ 1 ]
    Attribute "visibility" "photon" [ 1 ]
    Attribute "visibility" "transmission" [ "transparent"
]
    Patch "bilinear" "P" [ -5 -1 -5
                            5 -1 -5
                           -5 -1  5
                            5 -1  5 ]
WorldEnd
```

The "indirect" shader in Listing 30.8 adds the result of indirect-diffuse() into a standard lighting calculation. It simply requires the position, orientation, and number of samples to use. As indirectdiffuse() is used to calculate lighting for matte surfaces it needs to fire a lot of rays to capture the lighting in all directions, but these rays are shared between neighboring surface points, speeding the process up. The results in Figure 30.5 (also Plate X) show soft color bleeding on the underside of the teapot where it reflects the ground plane.

Listing 30.8 Indirect Diffuse.

```
surface indirect (float Kd=0.75;
                  float Kp=1;
                  float Ka=1;)
    {
    normal Nf=faceforward(normalize(N),I);
    Oi=Os;
    Ci=Cs*(Kd*diffuse(Nf)
        +Ka*ambient()
        +Kp*indirectdiffuse(P,Nf,100))*Oi;
    }
```

FIGURE 30.5. Indirect diffuse illumination (also Plate X)

Alternatively you can create an indirectdiffuse light shader which collects the light on behalf of the surface, and apply this light to standard shaders.

Caustics

In addition to handling diffuse reflections, photon maps are also well suited to handling caustics–highly complex light paths made up of multiple specular refractions or reflections. In these cases, the problem is that the paths may be very hard to find, but carry a lot of light. By starting at the light source we can "follow the energy." While regular photon maps will include caustics, you can specifically tell the renderer to seek out caustic lighting paths and store them in a separate photon map, during the map generation phase. This is done by replacing :

```
Attribute "photon" "globalmap" [ "photon.gpm" ]
```

With

```
Attribute "photon" "causticmap" [ "caustic.cpm" ]
```

You can specify both a causticmap and a globalmap to be generated in the same render pass, but generating them seperatly allows you to tune the number of photons used for each map.

Once this map has been generated we can use it just as we did the regular photonmap. However, as the caustic map only includes light which has bounced off (or refracted through) specular surfaces we need to add in the regular lighting. A simple shader which does this is shown in Listing 30.9.

Listing 30.9 A shader for using caustic maps.

```
surface causticPhoton (float Kd=0.75;
                float Kp=1;
                float Ka=1;
                string mapname="photon.cpm")
    {
    normal Nf=faceforward(normalize(N),I);
    Oi=Os;
    Ci=Cs*(Kd*diffuse(Nf)
        +Ka*ambient()
        +Kp*photonmap(mapname,P,Nf))*Oi;
    }
```

To generate Figure 30.6 (also Plate X) we applied a glass shader to the sphere, and generated a caustic map. When the final scene is rendered with the "causticPhoton" shader applied to the ground plane, the caustic map produces the bright spot in the centre of the sphere's shadow.

FIGURE 30.6. Caustics (also Plate X)

Rather then explicity using a photon map to generate caustics, you can also use the function `caustic(P,Nf)` which will use the map specified in the RIB file with:

```
Attribute "photon" "causticmap" [ "caustic.cpm" ]
```

Like `indirectdiffuse()` illumination caustics can be calculated in either a surface or light shader.

Summary

While it is tempting to think the GI is something that is simply "turned on," to get the best from it you must use each approach sparingly, combined with standard local illumination, depth mapped shadows and environment maps. By applying GI only where necessary you can save time on simple parts of the scene, and leaving more time to render the things which are important. Each of the illumination techniques available in RenderMan provides part of the solution to a difficult puzzle—to produce realistic images on a practical timescale.

As ray tracing and photon maps are some of the more recent features added to the RenderMan interface it is implementation is still in flux. Here we have described the basic interface, but most of the functions have additional options, which are implementation dependant. Some renderers may not support any of the GI features, while others may require slightly different commands to render the scene using GI. This will be described in your renderers documentation.

```
Attribute "visibility" "camera" [ 1 ]
Attribute "visibility" "trace"  [ 0 ]
Attribute "visibility" "photon" [ 0 ]
```
The "visibility" attribute controls whether geometry is considered when calculating camera rays, secondary traced rays, or photon maps.

```
Attribute "visibility" "transmission" ["transparent"]
Attribute "visibility" "transmission" ["opaque"]
Attribute "visibility" "transmission" ["Os"]
Attribute "visibility" "transmission" ["shader"]
```
The "transmission" visibility controls how an object interacts with ray-traced shadows. It is slightly more complex, as the object may be transparent, opaque, uniformly semi-opaque, or arbitrarily semi-opaque as defined by the shader.

```
Ctrans=transmission(Psrc,Pdest)
```
Tests the visibility between two points.

```
Chit=trace(P,dir);
```
Finds the color of the scene in direction dir from point P.

```
gather("illuminance", P, dir, angle, samples,
       "surface:Ci", Chit,...)
    {...} else { ... }
```
Traces a number of rays in a cone from the point P in direction dir. Upon a hit, the surface is interrogated, and the result made available in the first code block. If a ray fails to hit anything the second block is executed.

```
Option "trace" "maxdepth" [ 10 ]
Attribute "trace" "maxspeculardepth" [ 2 ]
```
If ray tracing were to be allowed to continue indefinitely some scenes might never be rendered. Maxdepth is the absolute limit on how deep rays can be traced, while maxspeculardepth provides a per object limit.

```
d=raylevel()
```
Counts the number of bounces from the camera to the current ray.

```
Hider "photon" "emit" [ 10000000 ]
```
Specifies that the current render pass should generate a global or caustic photon map, rather than a final image.

```
Attribute "photon" "globalmap" [ "photon.gpm" ]
Attribute "photon" "causticmap" [ "photon.cpm" ]
```
During the photon map generation pass these RIB commands sepecify if a caustic and/or global photon map should be generated, and the file names that should be used. During a render pass the maps specified are used by functions like `indirectdiffuse()` and `caustic()` which implicitly access photon maps.

```
Cp=photonmap("photon.pmap",P,Nf,...)
```
Interrogates a photon map to find the light hitting a surface with orientation `Nf` at point `P`.

```
Cid=indirectdiffuse(P,Nf,10)
Attribute "trace" "maxdiffusedepth" [ 1 ]
```
`Indirectdiffuse()` calculates bounce lighting for a surface, by tracing a specified number of rays. `Maxdiffusedepth` provides a limit to the depth of rays traced. Once this limit is reached the global photon map is used to complete the calculation.

```
Cc=caustic(P,Nf,...)
```
Calculates caustic lighting for the point `P`.

Bibliography

Four publications cover most of the information required to make successful use of a RenderMan renderer. Anyone seriously interested in rendering will eventually end up owning these books. They all assume a relatively high level of technical ability, and cover a lot of material very quickly. However, if you've worked your way through this book then you should be able to tackle them without too much difficulty.

RenderMan Companion, A Programmer's Guide to Realistic Computer Graphics, (Steve Upstill), Addison Wesley, 1990

For most RenderMan users this is the primary source of information. It covers modeling and shading in great detail. It is, however, based on the original RenderMan standard, and as such has a number of omissions. Most obviously the book was written before the introduction of RIB files, and hence discusses RenderMan purely in terms of the C API. While adapting the information to RIB is usually trivial, it does make the book difficult to follow for weaker programmers.

Advanced RenderMan (Apodaca & Gritz), Morgan Kaufmann, 1999

This book starts at a simple level, and provides a moderately good reference section covering both RIB and shading Language. It also includes a tutorial section covering much of the maths and physics of rendering. However, it moves quickly from this introduction to more complex topics. As such it does live up to its "Advanced" title.

The RenderMan Standard v3.2 (Pixar) 2000

This document, available as a PDF from Pixar's website (www.pixar.com), formally defines the RenderMan API including all the extensions and features added by Pixar up until the time of its publication. As such it provides a level of detail unmatched elsewhere, including details of features which are not supported even by Pixar's renderer. However, the price for this accuracy is a text which few users would choose to read. If you need to know exactly how something works then this is the place to look, but for most purposes refer to the previous texts.

Texturing and Modelling: A Procedural Approach (Ebert et al), Academic Press, 1998

This is not book about RenderMan as such, but a broader guide to the concepts of procedural texturing. However, most of the ideas can be implemented in SL, or are already built into the language. The format of the book is a collection of chapters written by a number of authors, which makes it a little inconsistent at times, and the academic style may seem off putting, but the quality of information makes this an essential book which you will return to many times.

Index